RACQUETBALL:
STRATEGIES FOR WINNING

Lou Fabian

RACQUETBALL: STRATEGIES FOR WINNING

Lou Fabian

Department of Health, Physical, and Recreation Education
University of Pittsburgh
Pittsburgh, Pennsylvania 15261

eddie bowers publishing company
2884 HICKORY HILL
DUBUQUE, IOWA 52001

eddie bowers publishing company
2884 HICKORY HILL
DUBUQUE, IA 52001

ISBN 0-912855-65-7

Printed in the United States of America.

9 8 7 6 5 4 3 2 1

DEDICATION

To my dear wife, Sue, for her extreme patience and good humor during my countless hours of racquetball practice and play, and the writing of this book.

To Molly O'Brien, Marcy Lynch, Kerry Niggemyer, and Al Plummer for the help and expertise they provided this author.

To Marc Haberman for his superb photography and to Steve Ballash and Marilyn Ross for appearing in the photographs contained herein.

To Marge Van Tassel and Sue Singer for their assistance with editing, and in preparing all tables and diagrams.

To Fran Ceravolo, Herb Meyers, Al Schattner and Gene Grapes, for their tremendous support and friendship during my years of learning racquetball.

And, to the many racquetball players I have played with and watched, from novice to top professional, men and women alike, who have given me the material to produce this book.

ABOUT THE AUTHOR

LOU FABIAN has taught racquetball for more than 13 years, during which time he served as Head Pro, Program Director and General Manager for OFF THE WALL HEALTH & FITNESS CLUBS in Pennsylvania.

Mr. Fabian holds a B.S. and an M.S. in Health and Physical Education from the Pennsylvania State University; since 1974, he has been on the faculty of the University of Pittsburgh. Mr. Fabian is a professional instructor certified by the American Professional Racquetball Organization; he is also a Level I Official with the American Amateur Racquetball Association. He has been a State Director for the AARA and has served on the Board of Directors for APRO.

Mr. Fabian was head Racquetball Instructor at the first Olympic Development Championships held in Colorado Springs, Colorado. He has written more than fifty (50) articles on Racquetball, Sports and Recreation and has coached top amateurs and women professionals, as well as hundreds of players of all ages and levels of ability.

TABLE OF CONTENTS

PREFACE

The purpose of this book is to accomplish something which has never been done before. Included is an indepth presentation of the key phases of the game of racquetball. I begin at the serve and end with how to think like a winner. The book takes a microscopic look at each of the major phases of the game. Although when viewed from the outside, racquetball is seen as a chaotic hit-and-run game, once the game is broken down into its constituent parts, racquetball is seen to contain as much form and strategy as other sports. To be a winner in this game, you must start with the basics and work toward mental mastery. A lot of practice and losses in tournament play can be incorporated into your overall development and help you to arrive at the goal of better stroke mechanics, good form, smart strategy, and the joys of winning against fine opposition. This book is intended to provide you with the basic stroke mechanics, practice drills, and winning strategies which will allow players of all levels to achieve their limits.

The game of racquetball can be viewed from a dual perspective; the serve and the rally. With this in mind, evaluate the opponent's game as to which area — the serve or the rally — is stronger or weaker. A simple strategy can be employed to defeat your opponent, neutralize his/her strength, and exploit relative weaknesses. For example, if your opponent has a dominant serve which relies on aces and setups to win, you should simply play a defensive return. If your opponent has a serve which attempts to force a rally, return their serves offensively.

To win in racquetball, you must begin with a sound serve. Indeed, the serve begins the rally and is usually the dominant force in most matches. To the casual observer, beginning and intermediate players, the serve is viewed as a means to initiate the rally. On the contrary, the advanced player and touring professional uses the serve to end the rally.

PART I of this book describes the serve in a depth and with a degree of completeness no other text has before. I detail five serves; the drive, Z, jam, lob, and the overhead Z. Each serve is described as to form, technique, strategy, position, serve variations, and deception. The material presented will explain the relevance of each serve in relationship to the game as a whole. I also have valuable suggestions on how to practice, and develop the necessary skills to win.

My second major perspective on racquetball — the rally — is detailed in **PART II** of this book. The text will detail the various ways to win the rally, specifically, middle court play, the return of serve, and back wall play. These areas are covered in detail and include strategies, the correct form, shot selection, drills, and the common errors from each court position.

Every sport has a mental component which requires study and practice for improvement. In fact, racquetball's combative one-on-one nature provides each player with many opportunities to experience each aspect of the mental game. **PART III** of this book will describe each of the mental aspects of racquetball. Areas of discussion will include anticipation, concentration, mental practice, and flow.

These topics cover the entire range of mental preparation which is necessary to make much improvement in your game. Specifically, anticipation details how to prepare for a match, how to deceive your opponent with your serves, and anticipation during the rally from each specific area of the court. Concentration deals with improving your ability to focus on the ball and describes techniques to employ both on and off the court. Mental practice involves on-and-off court tasks which will improve your form, serves, and return of serve. Flow is the ultimate level of the mental game, attainable only by the most devoted students.

Improving the mind and body are more important to the champion than winning. Self-improvement in each area will lead to winning games. Specifically, practicing like a champion, scouting an opponent correctly, using the information to develop a winning strategy, and thinking-utilizing brain power over brawn — this is the legacy of championship doubles. The characteristics of a champion include drive, desire, hard work, and concentration. These qualities must come from within yourself and will stay long after your last rollout. The essence of **PART IV** is to show the reader some valuable lessons of life which can be learned by playing racquetball.

My goal is to focus on blending the strategy of mind and body on the racquetball court. I hope that, my book will provide new insights for players of each ability level to improve performance. This information has been tested and proven by top amateurs, racquetball professionals, and by me. The topics presented here will certainly improve your racquetball game, and can also affect other areas of your life in a positive way. The book is on four levels; beginning, intermediate, advanced, and teaching professional. The material is presented clearly and simply, and when combined with the illustrations and drills should provide a complete approach to the game of racquetball.

Contact Zone.

CHAPTER 1

THE DRIVE SERVE

The serve is the only area in racquet-ball where a player has the opportunity to be completely in control. The key elements of success are present in each and every serve. These elements include **WHEN** the ball will be served, **WHERE** the ball will be served, and **WHAT** serve will be used. How or in what manner the ball will be served, and who (in doubles) will be the receiver are also crucial factors in playing racquetball to win. Accordingly, the player who best controls the serve will be in control and will very probably win the game! This chapter provides the reader with information necessary to make decisions about the use of the drive serve.

The **DRIVE SERVE** is the most popular serve in racquetball today. Many accomplished players build their service games around this serve. If you can make the ball bounce just past the short line, and not hit the side and back walls, you will minimize the effective returns of even the strongest of opponents. The main objective of the serve is to force the opponent to play your ball on the run. The consistent application of pressure with an effective drive serve will require model form, proper starting positions, correct frontwall targeting, and mental practice with your serve.

WHERE TO START

Model form is defined as a repeatable swing that allows consistent and powerful drive serves. Erratic form will cause the ball to be long, short, or hit the side wall for an easy kill by the opponent. This discussion of form begins with the server's position in the service box (see Diagram 1-1). Position yourself 2 to 3 ft. left of center in the service box (if you are right-handed). The exact position will vary for each player because the objective is to allow the sweet spot of the racquet to pass through the contactpoint of your shot on every serve you make. Use the visual cues present on the court to help you find the midpoint of the short line (i.e. position of the lights, the door if it is in the center of the back wall, and panel lines on the court walls). This midcourt position will

enable you to serve to either side of the court. It also allows room for the ball to pass your body, permitting you to retain advantage in center court (see Diagram 1-2). Your feet should be staggered (left in front of right) and touching (not over) the short line (see Picture 1-1). Right-handed players face the right side wall, with knees bent enough so that when fully extended during the swing, you can add power to the ball. Your upper torso should be bent at the waist and should remain bent until you follow through. This will help your control by keeping the racquethead on a level plane as you swing through the contact point. Maximum control will soon be mastered.

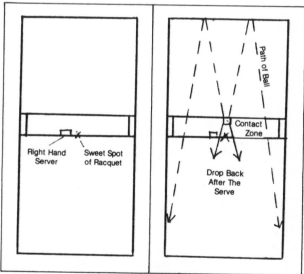

Diagram 1-1. *Server's Position in Service Box.*

Diagram 1-2. *Path of Serve and Drop Back After Serve.*

The racquet (forehand grip with cocked wrist) is held in the right hand and the ball in the left hand. Together, they are aligned with the sweet spot of the racquet and directly below your eyes (see Picture 1-1).

THE SWING

The swing uses a two-step motion. First, the right foot (back foot) initiates the swing with a short step toward the front wall (9 to 12

Photo 1-1. *Feet Staggered and Touching Short Line. Hands Aligned With Sweet Spot of Racquetball.*

Photo 1-2. *Back Swing.*

inches). Second, the left foot takes a full stride and moves in the direction you want the serve to go (see Pictures 1-2). Simultaneously, with your first step, your right arm is taken back for the back swing to about shoulder-high, and your left arm should move forward to drop the ball into the contact zone.

At this point in your swing, it is very important to understand that your body's muscles, joints, and ligaments will naturally move in a powerful sequence to generate a very strong and quick serve. Power is a combination of momentum and direction. All of your energy must be channeled in the direction of the serve. As the left leg takes a full stride into the shot, the hips will rotate forward with the step. The upper torso should remain bent through the shot, while the shoulders lead the rotation through the swing. As your shoulders lead the swing, your left arm should rotate out of the way. Don't ever take your eye off the ball. Ideally, your right arm follows the shoulder rotation to the ball. As the arm swing comes forward, your elbow extends fully and the wrist is broken as you follow through the ball's contact zone (see Pictures 1-3 & 1-4).

The contact zone is the area near the front of the service box, in direct alignment with your arm swing (see Picture 1-5). The ball was dropped to land in the contact zone on a bounce and to be contacted at approximately

Photo 1-3. *Arm Swing, Elbow and Wrist.*

4

Photo 1-4. *Keep Your Eye on Ball and Stay Low.*

Photo 1-5. *Contact Zone.*

3" to 6" high. Remember to time your swing so that you strike the ball at its apex with a fully extended wrist-break.

    Strive to hit the ball with 85% power; this gives you maximum control and also saves energy that you might need later. Repeating the

same swing is necessary for consistency; repetition also helps you avoid telegraphing your intentions. If you can repeat the same motion every time and you are still unable to retain the service, look for any inconsistency in your ball drop with regard to the point of contact.

    Your follow-through should be as natural and compact as possible, with your eyes following the ball all the way to the front wall target zone and back across the short line. As the ball strikes the front wall, you should shift your weight backwards in the direction of your relocation position (see Diagram 1-2). Push off the left leg (front leg) to begin the transfer of your weight. Your right foot should never leave the ground during the sequence of your swing, its follow-through, or the transfer of your weight from one side to the other (see Pictures 1-6). Practice your swing, follow through, and relocate after the serve without the ball. Concentrate completely on both your form and your position.

Photo 1-6. *Follow Through.*

    If you have any difficulty dropping back, it is probably because your strides are too long. Shorten your stride and concentrate on better balance. When you relocate, your right foot acts as the pivot foot, and your left foot leads the movement out of the service box. Your body should remain low throughout this entire movement. Diagram 1-2 indicates the direction line for proper setup after the serve.

SETUP AFTER THE SERVE

    As your body moves backward, look off the ball and read the opponent, positioning yourself for a low or high return according to his/her actions. If you see a low return coming, stop your movement and reverse direction for a

Photo 1-7. *Low Return Coming.*

Photo 1-8. *High Return Coming.*

forward or lateral change (see Picture 1-7). Keep your racquet low, and in front of your body, with your wrist cocked. Take a lunge step or cross-over step toward the ball and rekill it in the nearest corner. If you see a high return coming, continue the body movement toward the back wall. Gradually, you must rise out of this low body position and keep your racquet back, anticipating your opponent's next shot (see Picture 1-8). Your opponent's position will always dictate the selection of your next shot. In general, if the opponent is deep, hit an offensive shot, and if the opponent is in center court, hit a defensive shot. If you served to your backhand side of the court, then you should have switched to a backhand grip. A good time to do this is at the end of the follow-through after the serve; with practice, it is a natural motion.

TARGET YOUR SERVES

Success at the most advanced level of racquetball requires pinpoint accuracy of your serve. The slightest error in your serve can result in a setup for the opponent and a side-out for you. Four things can help you to minimize error and force the opponent to play your ball on the run. These include model form, a precise starting position, front wall targeting, and a lot of mental practice.

STARTING POSITIONS AND FRONT WALL TARGETS

The starting position for a drive serve to either side of the court is for your racquethead to be at the midpoint of the serve box (10 ft. from the side wall), with your feet on the short

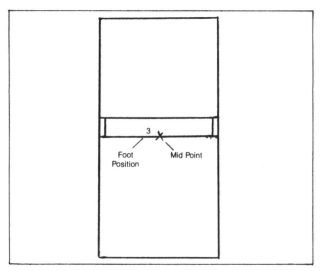

Diagram 1-3. *Position #3 for drive serve.*

6

line. For reference, we will label this position #3 (see Diagram 1-3). From position #3, the beginning player should master the drive serve to both sides of the court. Remember, the drive serve must not carom off the side or back walls. Intermediate players should perfect drive serves from position #3 to the four corners of the service area (see Diagram 1-4). For reference, the corners are labeled left near corner (LNC), left far corner (LFC), right near corner (RNC), and right far corner (RFC). Diversity in serving gives you more opportunity to exploit your opponent's weaknesses and hamper the receiver from easily returning your serve.

When all four serves are mastered from position #3, move the starting position and relearn the entire series. Additional positions are shown in Diagram 1-5 and measured as follows: position #1, straddling the short line where it connects with the left doubles box line; position #2, is midway between #1 and #3, standing on the short line; position #4 is midway between #3 and #5, standing on the short line; and position #5 — standing so the sweet spot of the racquet is on the short line where it meets the right side doubles box line. Place

tape on the short line to use as a guide when practicing, and, above all, warm up before a match from all five positions.

The main reason of this type of service game is keeping your opponent off balance; it also helps you to achieve greater flexibility in your service game. For example; suppose your opponent's greatest weakness is the drive serve to the backhand and the opponent begins to handle your serve because you have only been serving from position #3. Do not change your serve to a lob or Z, which you know your opponent can handle. Instead, switch your drive serve position. From these five positions, you can have up to ten drive serves to the backhand in your repertoire (see Table 1-1).

Position #1 and #5 require a slight modification in your form, due to the acute angle of the serve. If you are right-handed, walk out one or two steps from position #1, then angle your entire body movement in the direction of the serve to change direction and also maintain your power. From position #5, the right-hander may back up a step before changing directions toward the serve. Generally speaking, the direction of the serve is altered by your entire body motion and/or the ball toss. Some players think this is telegraphing; however, from the wide spectrum of positions #1 and #5, the receiver cannot easily distinguish change of direction. Many people incorrectly use an arm swing or a wrist snap to change the direction of a serve, thus causing them to lose power consistency and accuracy.

The next area of discussion is the **SELECTION OF FRONT WALL TARGETS** for the drive serves. Many people have target boxes on the front wall. However, with 20 drive serves, as indicated earlier, the box would extend the entire width of the front wall. A simpler technique for beginners through advanced players to employ is taping a line on the front wall (see Diagram 1-6). Beginners would begin with a line at 18" high. Intermediate players would place

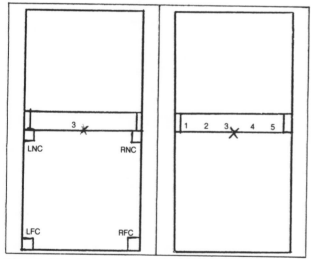

Diagram 1-4. *Four corners of service area.*

Diagram 1-5. *Drive serve starting positions.*

Table 1-1:	Drive Serves From Different Start Positions			
Position 1	LNCab	LFC	RNC	RFCa
Position 2	LNC	LFC	RNC	RFC
Position 3	LNC	LFC	RNC	RFC
Position 4	LNC	LFC	RNC	RFC
Position 5	LNC	LFC	RNCb	RFC

a Drive left near corner, Drive right far corner
b Serves which crack out for winners are points even if they are screens.

their line at 12" high, advanced players at 9" high, and professionals at 6" high. This sophisticated serving technique is best developed with one-half hour practice sessions, alone on the court, and with practice games (drive serves only) to seven points with a partner.

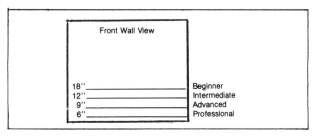

Diagram 1-6. *Front-wall target lines for drive serve.*

MENTAL PRACTICE

Generally speaking, the height of the ball on your drive serve is controlled by the height of contact, the plane of the racquet face, and the power you are able to give to the ball. The direction your ball takes depends upon the start position and the direction your body and the racquethead take. A front wall target point isn't always necessary if your starting point and body momentum are correct. You can't always tape targets on the wall during a match. You can, however, mentally practice the direction you want the ball to take after contact. Mental practice is the most important element necessary to perfect a powerful drive serve. Mental practice is simply the ability to envision in your mind's eye what you are going to make happen just before you hit the ball.

Begin by standing at position #1, ready to serve the ball (DRFC). Imagine with your eyes and your mind a dotted line to the front wall target line and back across the short line to the spot on the floor where you want the serve to end. Serve the ball along this imaginary dotted line. Repeat your service until the ball finishes where you want it to. This mental practice should be repeated for all four serves from all five positions.

The value of the preparation of mental practice must be stressed! A half-hour practice session on the court twice a week will improve your service game dramatically!

Aspiring players should use this mental practice off the court to refine their racquetball skills even further. This technique is simple, and only requires 20 minutes three times a week. In a quiet room, begin by sitting or lying in a comfortable position. Close your eyes and imagine yourself entering a racquetball court going to position #1 and setting up to serve the ball.

Repeat the following procedure for all serves from all positions:
1. Imagine looking at a receiver (preferably someone better than you) and select a serve to defeat the receiver's position.
2. Serve the ball and see it clear the short line for an ace.
3. After you serve the ball, drop into a setup position behind the short line and on the side of the court where the ball was served.
4. Anticipate what shot the receiver would have hit had he/she retrieved the ball and take a position to rekill the third shot for a winner.

Champion players mentally practice these situations while they are playing a match during the 10 seconds they have before serving. The following section elaborates on what to look for in the receiver's position and what serves to select.

EXPLOIT WHAT IS GIVEN

Select a serve which exploits the receiver's position. Given the ability that you can serve the ball to any point in the receiving area, select a serve which makes the opponent run the furthest. Therefore, the first task upon entering the service box is to look at the receiver's position. Do not select the serve or position of the serve until you have done this.

In general, five situations will occur and can be countered:
1. The receiver sets up in the center court four feet off the back wall (center) (see Diagram 1-7).
2. The receiver sets up left of center (see Diagram 1-8).
3. The server sets up right of center (see Diagram 1-9).
4. The receiver sets up 8 to 10 ft. from the back wall (see Diagram 1-10).
5. The receiver sets up 2 ft. from the back wall (see Diagram 1-11).

Select a serve which makes the receiver run the furthest. Do not be timid about serving to the receiver's forehand. A well-executed serve to the receiver's forehand, if the receiver is out of position, will result in a winner.

The five situations stated above correspond to the five diagrams shown. Remember, do not serve the same serve twice in a row; however, you have five positions to serve from. The shaded areas represent the target areas for your servers.

Granted, most opponents tend to cover their faults by shading to their weak side. They also see many more serves to their weak side. Look for information about the receiver's ability

8

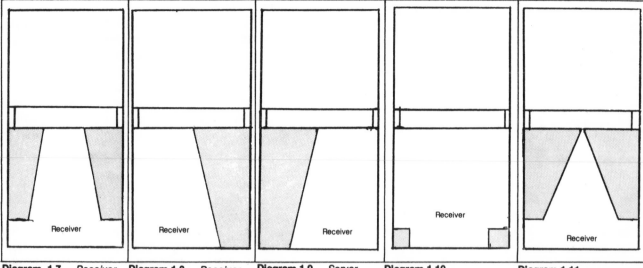

Diagram 1-7. *Receiver Sets Up in Center.*

Diagram 1-8. *Receiver Sets Up Left of Center.*

Diagram 1-9. *Server Sets Up Right of Center.*

Diagram 1-10. *Receiver Sets Up 8 to 10 ft. From Back Wall.*

Diagram 1-11. *Receiver Sets Up 2 ft. From Back Wall.*

to return the serve effectively on the run (the most difficult skill in racquetball). Learn how well your opponent moves laterally. How effective are they at moving forward and into the corners to retrieve your serve? How do they return from their forehand and backhand sides of the court? Most receivers hold a backhand grip for the return of the serve. These questions will enable you to better understand and plan a specific strategy to defeat your opponent.

Champion players always have the confidence and ability to "put the ball on a dime." They can also retrieve any service except the crack serve. The following section provides information on outsmarting the physically gifted player with finesse. Topics include misdirection drive serves, shadowing the serve, a power service motion, the change-up drive serve, slicing the serve, and setting up the receiver with three serve combinations.

MISDIRECTION DRIVE SERVE

A misdirection drive serve is a serve which causes the receiver to start his/her body movement in one direction and then forces him/her to change direction to play the ball. Diagram 1-12 shows a normal drive serve from position #4, then a misdirection drive serve from position #4. The path of the ball begins in the direction of the backhand corner, but strikes the side wall 34' to 36' back, and angles toward the center.

Another type of misdirection serve is shown in Diagram 1-13. These are drive serves up the middle that work when the receiver breaks away from the middle at the serve's

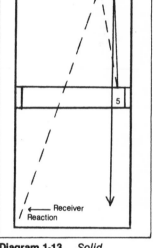

Diagram 1-12. *Normal Drive Serve.* — — — — *Misdirection Drive Serve.* ——————

Diagram 1-13. *Solid Line - Misdirection Drive Serve Towards Middle Court. Dotted Line - Normal Drive Serve.*

onset. This is best accomplished after you have served several normal drive serves. At no time should a misdirection drive serve come off the back wall. Also, worthy opponents tend not to to fooled by the same trick twice in one game.

SHADOWING THE SERVE

Receivers often use a technique of looking through the served ball to the front wall to get a cue as to which side, forehand or backhand, the ball is being served. One way to counteract this is to alter the service motion so the ball is dropped and contacted in front of your body, i.e. shadowing the serve. You may trade off power to regain control as you practice this technique; however, delaying the receiver's reaction time to the serve is worth the trade-off. Another form of shadowing is caused by a walking or running motion by the server. This technique is most effective from positions #1 and #2.

THE POWER SERVICE MOTION

Many players experience a situation during a game when the score is tied 12-12 and both players have adjusted their body movements to the speed of the serve. The obvious solution is to change the speed of the serve; however, you may want to continue serving a drive serve in lieu of a lob serve. One answer is to use that 15% power that you have been holding in reserve. Most players have a tendency to overhit their serves and hand the receivers setups.

A method of guarding against this mistake is to alter your normal horizontal stroke to a power vertical stroke! If practiced correctly, you will be able to hit your service just as accurately this way. The reason you do not want to use this power stroke throughout an entire match is because it takes a lot of the strength and energy out of your arm and shoulder. A simple analogy would be the short relief pitcher in baseball that the coach brings in during the late innings of a game to throw smoke at the batters. The relief pitcher could not sustain this performance for an entire game.

The power stroke is altered by rising from the crouch position and extending the serving arm above your head. Bring your arm down through the ball with your maximum velocity. This will increase the arc length and add significant power to your ball. The timing of this stroke is changeable; therefore, practice subtle adjustments in the rest of your form as necessary. The power service motion is coincidentally very effective with the misdirection drive serve because less accuracy is required in this serve.

CHANGE UP DRIVE SERVE

The second method of changing speeds on the receiver is to slow the ball down. The end result is the same — the serve clears the service line, and doesn't carom off the side or back walls. However, the slower speed throws the receiver's timing off and consequently forces a weak return (if the ball is returned at all).

The basic service motion remains unchanged, even though the ball is contacted at a higher-than-normal level. The normal stroke should contact the ball between 3" and 6" high, while the change-up drive serve should be contacted at between 9" and 12" high. In lieu of 85% power, the force should be reduced to 50%. Perfection of the change-up drive serve will require many hours of practice. Several suggestions include practicing the change-up drive serve continuously, until perfected, then practicing a normal drive serve followed by a change-up drive serve. Perfect the change-up drive serve to your forehand side before ever trying it to your backhand side. The change in direction to your backhand greatly compounds the serve's difficulty. Therefore, limit your practice to positions #4 and #5 to the right side and #1 and #2 to the left side.

SLICING THE SERVE

Previously, we have discussed altering the direction and speed of the serve. One element remains to be explored and that is getting spin on the ball. The normal stroke should put little or no spin on a drive serve. The effects of top spin and bottom spin on the drive serve have little advantage, if any, and should not be practiced. However, top and bottom spins on certain shots during the rally are effective. Side spin can only be placed across the face of the ball in one direction when serving drive serves — left side spin for the right-handed player and right side spin for the left-handed player. Also, slicing specific drive serves can be very effective! These include drive serves to the left from positions #1 and #2 and drive serves to the right from positions #4 and #5, (because the action caused by spin as the ball touches the side walls). Balls served and sliced to the left by the right-hander will hug the side wall, while balls served and sliced to the right side by the right-hander will kick out when the spin grabs the wall. The variety of actions caused by slicing the drive serve will continue to keep the receiver off balance. A word to the wise — if the courts are dusty, slicing the drive serve can really frustrate your opponent and destroy his/her concentration and composure.

Another technique difficult-to-execute which is very frustrating to the receiver is spinning the ball so much on the drop that it kicks away from you just before you hit it. Most receivers are watching the ball bounce to the right as you serve it back to the left. The advantage to this is that you can gain a split-second of time when the receiver watches the ball's motion. The disadvantage of this ploy is that you sacrafice accuracy.

The practice and combination of all types of serves will help make and keep you a champion. Your ability to exploit the receiver's weaknesses and create weaknesses where none exist are the skills which must be developed to win matches in tournament racquetball.

CREATE A WEAKNESS

When the receiver has no apparent weaknesses on the return of service, you must create weaknesses for him/her. By employing the serves described previously, you can manipulate and set the receiver up into weaker returns. Two situations commonly exist which are exploitable. First, the receiver repeatedly returns the same shot. This enables you to select the serve which makes that return more difficult and immediately setup for a third shot which you anticipate. Before serving, however, mentally practice setting up for the third shot and successfully putting the ball away.

The second situation is your ability to keep the receiver off balance with three serve combinations. A three-serve combination is usually three first serve attempts, not a 1st and 2nd serve situation. The three-serve combination deceives your opponent. His/her initial reaction shifts his/her weight the wrong way, enabling you to score points. The number of combinations is endless, and only your ability and imagination limit you.

The following lists are common three-shot drive serve combinations:
1. Drive left far corner, position #3
   Drive left near corner, position #2, change up
   Misdirection drive left, position #5, power stroke
2. Drive left far corner, position #3
   Drive right far corner, position #3
   Drive left near corner, position #3
3. Drive right far corner, position #4
   Misdirection drive right side, position #4
   Drive right near corner, position #5, slice
4. Drive right far corner, position #1
   Drive left near corner, position #1, slice
   Misdirection drive left side, position #1
5. Drive left far corner, position #5
   Misdirection drive — left side, position #5, power stroke
   Misdirection drive — right side, position #5

These are only a few combinations — imagine what you can do when you include Z and Jam serves in your repertoire!

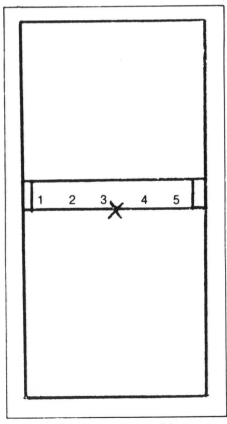

Drive serve starting positions.

11

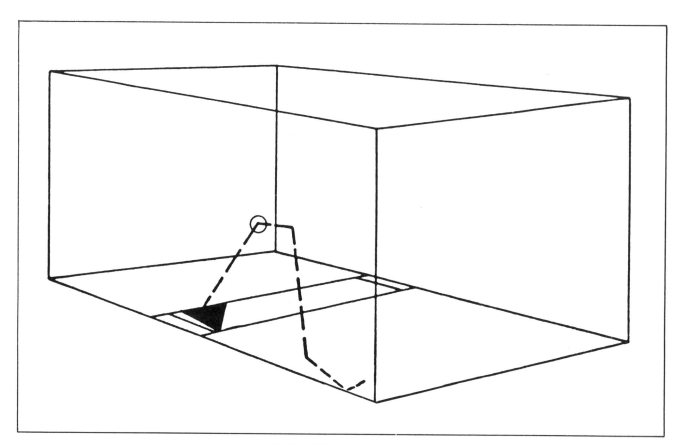

Path and Bounce of Z-Serve.

CHAPTER 2

THE Z-SERVE

Two months before the 1971 National Racquetball Championships, Charlie (The Gar) Garfinkel was on the court experimenting with different types of serves. He noticed that if he started from a set position in the service box and consistently placed the serve in a visualized target area, the ball would take wild and unpredictable bounces off the side wall. Two months later, in April, during the second round of the Nationals, Garfinkel discovered just how effective the new serve could be.

The Gar was playing Charlie Brumfield, the 2nd ranked player in the world, and doing poorly. The Gar lost the first game 21-11 and fell behind rapidly 13-4 in the second game. At that point, he switched to his new serve and turned the match around.

Brumfield had so much trouble handling the unfamiliar bounces coming off the side wall that he was unable to return the serve with his usual precision. This slight edge earned Garfinkel many easy points and, ultimately, the match. The Gar had given Brumfield, racquetball's premier tactician, a resounding lesson in athletic creativity through his use of what the fans coined, "The Garfinkel Serve." Today this innovation is known as the Z-serve.

The **PURPOSE OF THE Z-SERVE** is to keep the receiver in back court, neutralize his/her power by preventing a full-arm swing, and limit his/her effectiveness and return by forcing the receiver to play the ball waist high in a corner. The advantages of accurate Z-serves includes: aces, weaker returns, prevention of the receiver from getting into a groove, and safety use for both serves. Unfortunately, the disadvantages of the Z-serve include: possible creation of plums for the receiver if the ball shoots straight out from the side wall or caroms off the back wall, and it can be effectively neutralized if the opponent moves up to cut it off down-the-line or crosscourt.

It should be noted that this chapter was written with the assumption that the server is right-handed. There are subtle differences in every racquetball environment (court, ball, etc.), each person's body type, and each person's athletic ability. "Be flexible!" Use this material as a general guideline with which to experiment and alter it when necessary. In addition, this chapter applies to beginning, intermediate, and advanced players, under the assumption that you realize there are no get-rich-quick schemes in racquetball. Both beginning and intermediate players must attain at least 90% proficiency at their respective levels before advancing to a higher level. If you fail to achieve 90% proficiency before advancing, you may have more frustrating moments rather than victories as a result.

BASICS OF THE Z-SERVE

The server should take a position within the shaded area of the service zone (see Diagram 2-1). Start with the right foot on the corner formed by the short line and doubles service box. It is important to begin at the same point each time you serve the ball. Also notice that the shaded area flares out from the starting point. This becomes very important when the server begins to change angles on different serves.

The **EXECUTION** of the Z-serve becomes easiest from the player's most left-of-center position. However, moving further to the left of center, increasingly telegraphs your intentions

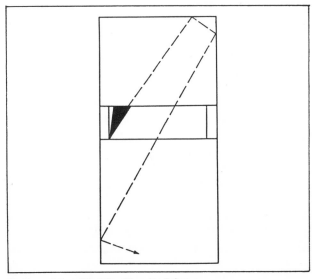

Diagram 2-1. *Start Position for Z-Serve.*

on the serve. Make an extra effort to return to center court position after each serve! Each player must experiment with different starting points on the short line to determine the exact position for best results.

Look at the receiver's position from your starting point; then decide what serve you want to hit. Find the appropriate target on the front wall and imagine yourself serving the ball to the target, and following it to the back court for an ace serve! This is called mental imagery, and sport scientists have proven that it will improve your accuracy.

The **STROKING PATTERN** for the Z-serve is similar to the pattern used for the drive serve, with one major difference: your body position is angled 45 degrees toward the right front corner rather than perpendicular to the front wall. Start your swing with your back foot, then step forward with your front foot toward the spot on the front wall where you want the ball to go. Using a forehand grip, make contact with the ball somewhere between ankle and knee height with 80% power. Think of the Z-serve as a drive serve in another direction. Once you begin your stroke, keep your eye on the ball, following it into the back court every time. Warning! You Must Wear Eye Protection!

Diagram 2-2, marks the server's target, an area approximately four feet above the floor and four feet away from the right side wall. Aim for this target, striking the ball, and following it as it caroms quickly off the front right side wall and angles crosscourt deep into the left corner. The ball must bounce on the floor prior to hitting the left side wall and then shoot off the side wall into the receiver's body (see Diagram 2-3).

Ideally, your serve will hit the left side wall one-to-four feet away from the back wall and three feet high (see Diagram 2-4). The bounce off the left side wall should be unpredictable. Sometimes the ball will drop, rise, shoot straight out, or angle toward the back wall. Be careful! If you do not hit your target, the ball will setup off the back wall or hit shallow and shoot straight out for a plum. This is why starting from the same point and perfecting the target angle is so important!

Setting up in the **PROPER CENTER COURT POSITION** after serving the ball is the next step toward perfecting your game. Failure to do this accounts for most losses by beginners. First, follow the ball past the short line (turning in the direction of the ball, approximately 270 degrees) to a position four-to-seven feet behind the short line shading left of center court, as in Diagram 2-5. Watch the path of the

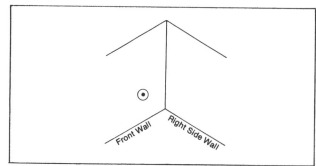

Diagram 2-2.   *Server's Target.*

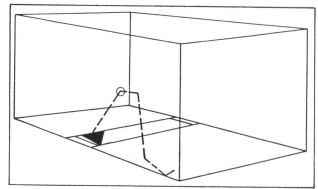

Diagram 2-3.   *Path and Bounce of Z-Serve.*

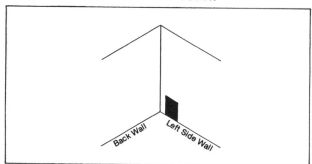

Diagram 2-4.   *Where Z-Serve Will Hit Side Wall.*

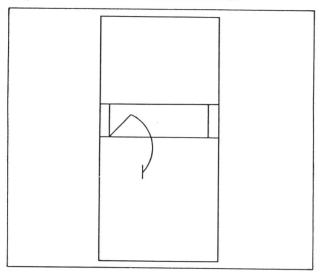

Diagram 2-5.   *Set-Up After the Serve.*

ball and determine whether the receiver will use the ceiling or an offensive return. Depending upon your style, switch the racquet to a backhand grip. While turning, setup with your racquet comfortably back.

Once in center court position, the server must be ready for any number of **RETURNS.** As I have described earlier, the server is in position to cover the down-the-line pass, straight kill, and straight ceiling ball. At the beginning level, these returns are all that you should be concerned with. Any other returns will be to your advantage and should set you up for an easy forehand shot! However, if the receiver does attempt to cut the ball off before it hits the side wall, you must cover both the pinch shot and crosscourt pass.

The receiver makes contact with the ball far in front of his/her body. Adjustments! Move your center court position toward midcourt, or hit your Z-serve harder so that the receiver cannot cut it off before the side wall. The beginning player must be able to hit the Z-serve accurately, and setup in the proper center court position 90% of the time. When you feel too confident, it is time to change levels!

EXPAND YOUR ARSENAL

The intermediate player must concentrate on developing a series of serves from the same spot with the same motion. Develop deception, use a quick, consistent motion but vary the angles, speeds, and height of your serve. Keep your opponent off balance! These variations should include the following serves: a change of pace Z-serve (approximately 50% power) which can also be used as a second serve; a drive serve deep into the right corner which can be used if the receiver either cheats to the left or moves before the ball is served; and a short angle drive to the left front service area which is very effective if the receiver sets up deep in the back court to get behind the Z-serve (see Diagram 2-6).

Diagram 2-7 shows front wall targets from the starting position, and Diagram 2-8 shows back court locations where the serve should fall. Of special note, the soft Z-serve should not reach the side wall before bouncing twice, thereby forcing the receiver to play it out of midair; the drive serve to the right corner must not carom off the right side wall; and, needless to say, neither drive serve should come off the back wall.

A game strategy for these four serves should be as follows: Of every 10 first serves, utilize six hard Z's, two short angle drives, one soft Z, and one crosscourt drive. A general rule of thumb would be never to use the same serve twice in a row. In addition to watching the receiver for a clue while in position, use one serve to setup another (i.e., hard Z then soft Z,

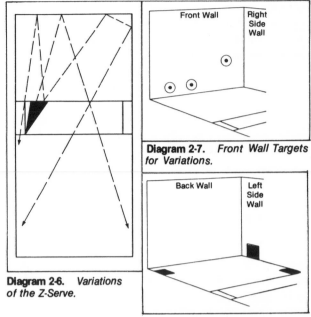

Diagram 2-6. *Variations of the Z-Serve.*

Diagram 2-7. *Front Wall Targets for Variations.*

Diagram 2-8. *Back Court Locations Where Ball Will Finish.*

hard Z then crosscourt drive, and then short angle drive).

The setup for center court position is similar for the soft Z-serve and, as stated previously, for the hard Z-serve. However, the drive serve dictates different setup positions. The crosscourt drive serve setup position should be three feet behind the short line and to the right of center court (see Diagram 2-9).

Maintain the forehand grip and take the racquet back by your right ear while running to that spot. The setup position for the short angle drive serve is different from the other serves because the server turns in the opposite direction (to the left), following the ball. As a general rule, drop back behind the short line (three

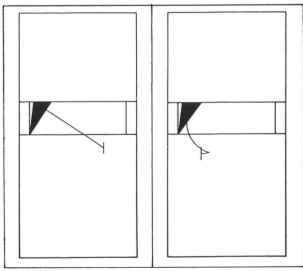

Diagram 2-9. *Setup Position to Cover the Crosscourt Drive Serve.*

Diagram 2-10. *Be Prepared for Return of Serve.*

feet deep), three feet left of center and be prepared (racquet back, proper grip, on your toes) when the receiver is about to return your serve (see Diagram 2-10).

Be less concerned with depth and width and more concerned about watching the ball and being ready to react. The intermediate player must be able to hit these serves with 90% accuracy. In addition, a constant motion must be perfected when serving. This helps to develop a deceptive strategy which must be measured before moving to the advanced level.

FORM A SERVING STRATEGY

You must realize that the serve and the setup after the serve are the decisive factors to winning racquetball games! Some readers probably wonder what makes the intermediate level more advanced? You should bear in mind that a successful tournament player has a complete service game developed around each of the five basic serves (lob, drive, Z, jam, and overhead Z) to either side of the court! That is ten different service games for singles alone.

The advanced player should perfect the serves pictured in Diagram 2-11. Short crosscourt and short angle drive serves are employed to force the receiver to retrieve the ball with the racquet in front of them, a position which will neutralize much of their power. The jam serve is an excellent weapon for your service arsenal; it is very deceptive and is employed a great deal in doubles. The jam serve (sometimes called body or diamond serve) is very effective when the receiver is a big person and

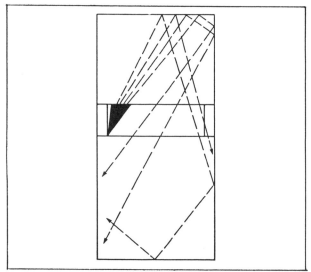

Diagram 2-11. *Advanced Variations of the Z-Serve.*

slow-footed; it is also particularly effective when the receiver is tired!

The hard Z deep and low to the corner is best when the receiver is waiting for the ball and looking for a setup. Diagram 2-11 shows these serves; Diagram 2-12 shows front wall targets; and Diagram 2-13 illustrates back court locations where the serves should fall.

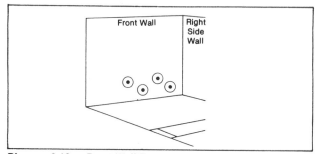

Diagram 2-12. *Front Wall Targets.*

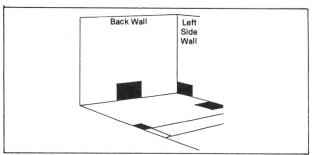

Diagram 2-13. *Back Court Locations the Ball Will Finish.*

One suggested game strategy for the eight serves is as follows: Of the first 20 serves,

    6 Hard Z's
    4 Short Angle Drives
    2 Soft Z's
    2 Hard Z's, Deep & Low to Corner
    2 Wide Jam
    2 Short Angle Z's
    1 Crosscourt Drive
    1 Short Crosscourt Drive

Remember!, never use the same serve twice in a row! Use one serve to set up the next. A practice technique which can be used by you and your partner is to have the receiver call which serve must be hit. This will force concentration on accuracy and all the variations.

Before playing a tournament match, warm-up on a court alone (preferably the court you are going to play on later). Practice your serves, though this may be difficult when your opponent is on the court warming up with you.

Mark your starting point on the short line. Decide beforehand which of the ten service games you are going to employ. During the first game, stay with your initial strategy. Use all eight serves without a particular order. Then, discard any serve that your opponent has adequately handled (not those poorly served by you). Form your serving strategy out of what has been most effective. If you have won the first game, stay with the same strategy. If you lose the first game, decide either to revise your serving strategy, or change serving positions (drive game to lob game).

What do you do against a left-handed opponent? Use the same eight serves perfected from a new starting point on the short line. Set-up about eight feet from the right side wall. Also, add an additional serve, the drive deep into the right corner.

Important! For the first time, watching the ball off the serve is not practical. All Z-serves to the right rear corner force the right-handed server to turn 360 degrees in order to follow them. It is much faster and safer to serve, then drop into center court position, and pick the ball up by looking over the right shoulder while in motion. As I have stated earlier, individual skill, style, and practice will require subtle variations in your game.

The previous chapter emphasized mastering five starting positions in the serving box. While variations of the Z and Jam serves can be mastered from all five positions, incorporation with the drive serve will provide you with a complete service game from each position. Practice three-serve combinations, then link three combinations together from one position. Try to establish your rhythm and run streaks of points. Remember, if the low-hard service game has been effective for you from position #3, and the opponent neutralizes it, try the same service game from another position before switching completely to high-soft service game.

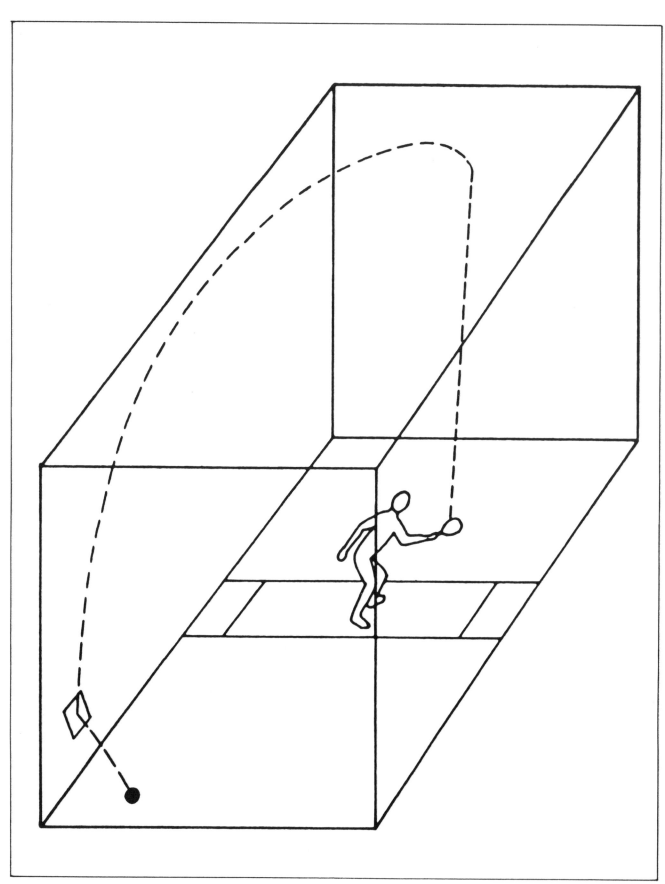

The High Lob Serve.

CHAPTER 3

THE LOB SERVE

The lob serve is the most misunderstood serve in racquetball. Many people believe the lob is reserved for beginners and second serves. In reality, the lob serve is a very effective weapon when used at the proper time. There is an important reason for using the lob serve against any type of racquetball player. The lob serve can be easily changed to counter every player's style! The lob can be used as a safety serve to put the ball in play or as an offensive weapon. If you select and execute the proper type of lob serve, you greatly increase the chances for opponent error, and, subsequently, you win the rally. This chapter explains the advantages and strategy of the lob serve, the proper form, serving elements, the types of lob serves, and serve selection.

STRATEGY

The primary advantage of the lob serve is to give you a service game to use for an entire match. The lob serve is excellent for changing the tempo of a game. When you discover a weakness in the opponent's return, the lob can be used to exploit it to the fullest. Never serve the same first or second serve twice in a row.

Use the lob serve to challenge the shooter! If the receiver waits to shoot the ball, serve a lob which finishes 38' deep in the backhand corner. If the receiver charges the lob to cut it off, serve high angled lobs or waist-high fast lobs. If the receiver plays the lob defensively, serve to the middle of the court, and the opponent will experience more difficulty in returning accurate ceiling balls. The lob serve should be used to change the tempo of the game when your drive serve is not working. The lob should be used to slow a faster player, neutralize the power player, and frustrate the short player. I will describe these and other lob serves, detailing the correct form, and outlining what you can expect from a well-executed lob service game.

LOB SERVE FORM

It would seem difficult, if not impossible, to disguise your intention to serve a lob serve, because of the upright body position required for execution. However, you can serve a variety of lob serves to keep the receiver off balance. Position yourself two feet left of center in the service box, facing the right side wall (if you're right-handed). Your right foot should be touching the short line and your feet shoulder-width apart (see Picture 3-1).

Begin your serve with the racquet and ball waist-high. Simultaneously, begin the ball drop 12 to 18 inches in front of your left foot and take a short backswing with your right arm. As the ball begins its upward bounce, bring the racquet forward meeting the ball at the apex of its bounce. The plane of the racquet at contact should **LIFT THE BALL.** As the racquet

Photo 3-1. *Right Foot Touching Short Line, Feet Shoulder-Width Apart.*

begins moving forward, step forward with the left foot. Keep your wrist stiff through the swing and follow through high in the direction you want the ball to travel. Be careful not to leave the service box before the ball crosses the short line (see Pictures 3-2 to 3-5).

Photo 3-4. *Racquet Contact Should Lift the Ball.*

Photo 3-2. *Step With Left Foot, Short Back Swing.*

Photo 3-3. *Meet Ball at Apex of Bounce.*

Photo 3-5. *Stiff Wrist and High Follow Through.*

Photo 3-6. *Drop Back, Push Off With Right Foot into Center Court.*

Photo 3-7. *Be Prepared to Cut Off Low Hard Return.*

Keep your eyes on the ball throughout the swing! You should look to the opponent immediately after the ball strikes the front wall to get an indication of how he/she intends to play the serve. Then drop back, push off with your right foot into the center court position about 25' to 27' deep, and favoring the side you served to (see Picture 3-6). If your opponent indicates a ceiling ball return, continue running toward the back wall. If opponent indicates a low return, turn to the left wall and, with a staggered step, bring your racquet waist-high with a backhand grip. Stay on your toes and be prepared to cut off a low hard return to either side of the court (see Picture 3-7).

SKILL ELEMENTS

Thus far, we have discussed good form and setting up after the lob serve. The following section details the elements and skills necessary to add variety to your lob serve game. Remember, your objective is to use the lob serve and keep the opponent off balance for an entire match. The key elements include; starting positions, height of the ball, speed of the serve, angle of the shot, and spin on the ball.

A precise starting position refers to the servers position in the service box at the beginning of the serve. Variety is accomplished by varying the position with five starting points. The positions shown in Diagram 3-1 indicate the starting points of the racquet, with the measurements being for the right-handed server, as measured from the left side wall. Starting position is crucial for variety because many variations of lobs can be served from each point.

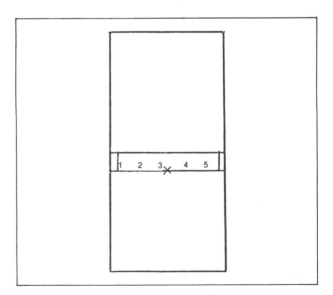

Diagram 3-1. *Start positions for Lob Serves.*

The second element needed for variety is height of the ball. Variety in height is necessary to make the receiver contact the serve at different heights in back court. Diagram 3-2 is a side view of the racquetball court and indicates the height for three types of lob serves. The variety in height forces the receiver to contact the ball at three different heights in back court.

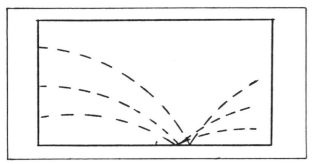

Diagram 3-2. *Height for 3 Types of Lob Serves (Side View).*

The element of speed is crucial to mastering the height of lob serves; too slow and the serve will be short, too fast and the serve will carry off the back wall for the receiver to kill. The combination of position, height, and speed should keep the receiver off balance, by forcing him/her to return the ball out of midair, from back court, without the serve hitting the side or back wall.

Until now, allowing the lob serve to touch the side wall has been a decided disadvantage for the server. Actually, at the higher levels of play, talented servers use the side wall to their advantage. The angle on the serve means using acute angles and the entire court to test the receiver's skill at returning serves accurately. For the first time, I advocate using the side wall for lob serves. Diagram 3-3 is a top view of the racquetball court and shows

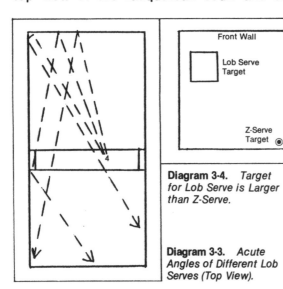

Diagram 3-4. *Target for Lob Serve is Larger than Z-Serve.*

Diagram 3-3. *Acute Angles of Different Lob Serves (Top View).*

acute angles of some lob serves. These serves are very difficult to return offensively and can create indecision within the receiver.

Spin is the last element I will discuss. The same serve will actually play differently if spin is used correctly on it. By slicing the ball to the left and serving to the right side, you will cause the ball to hug the side wall. Use underspin to cause the ball to bounce higher. Experiment with the various spins, and notice the reaction of the ball as it bounces and touches each wall. Combine spin, height, angle, position, and speed to keep the receiver off balance, to neutralize their power, minimize their offensive shots, and force inaccurate returns as setups for your next shot.

The objective of these lob serve elements is to make the receiver play the ball waist-to-shoulder high in back court. Since this is a large area, some flexibility in your front wall target is permissible (see Diagram 3-4). The best approach to placing the ball in this area is to look at the receiver, select a lob serve, imagine the ideal end position for the serve, then trace an imaginary line backwards at the proper height and angle to the front wall, and from the front wall target to your racquet. Now execute the serve and relocate into center court!

Thus far I have emphasized form, technique, and the elements necessary to master the lob serve. The final section describes specific types of lob serves. Players frequently have a narrow view of the types of lob serves; the following will describe orthodox and unorthodox lob serves.

TYPES OF LOB SERVES

The **HALF-LOB** Serve is the most widely used lob serve in racquetball today. It is the easiest to execute, but has the widest margin for error. Most beginners learn this serve their first time on a racquetball court, and many players use it as a second serve. The half-lob should finish 38' and deep within 6" of the side wall. The first bounce will occur around 24' off front wall in the safety zone. The front wall target is approximately 12' high (see Diagram 3-5). This end placement restricts the receiver's swing if they permit the ball to carry deep. To properly return the half-lob serve, the receiver should move forward and play the ball to the ceiling on the up bounce. The direction of the serve will vary slightly due to the starting position.

The **HIGH LOB** serve is very effective against the waiter and the impatient receiver.

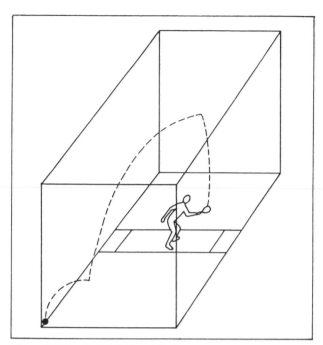

Diagram 3-5. *Half-Lob Serve Path.*

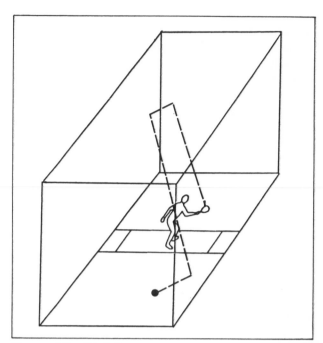

Diagram 3-7. *Z-Lob Serve.*

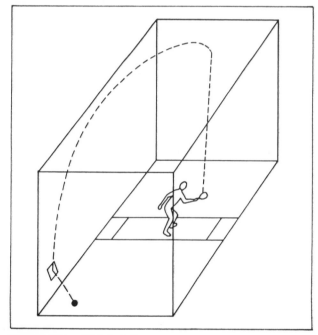

Diagram 3-6. *High Lob Serve.*

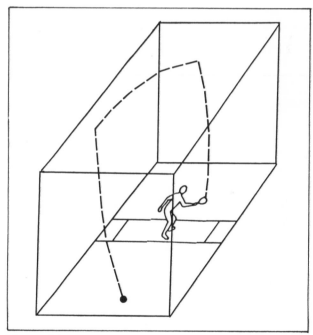

Diagram 3-8. *Trajectory of the Wide-Angle Lob Serve.*

The high lob serve should finish 38' deep but only after having **GRAZED THE SIDE WALL** at 36'. The serve should hit the front wall approximately 16' to 18' high. Diagram 3-6 depicts the high lob serve. A variation of the high lob is where the ball strikes the floor on the first bounce at 36', then bounces up to the side wall and finally settles at 39'.

The **Z-LOB** is the next most popular serve in the lob family. It can be served with either the forehand or backhand, from several positions in the service box to both sides of the court. The use of spin complements this serve immensely! The spin grabs nicely off the side wall. The served ball finishes in backcourt, with or without touching the second wall (see Diagram 3-7). Prior to bouncing in the safety zone, the ball strikes the front, then side wall of the racquetball court, anywhere from 8 to 18 feet high. Never let the Z-lob serve carom off the back wall! After touching the second side wall the ball should drop sharply to the floor. The Z-lob can be served from several positions with your backhand. This technique reverses the spin on the ball and allows you a better view of the receiver.

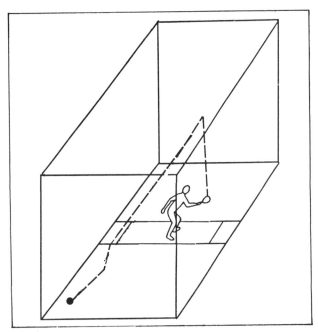

Diagram 3-9. *Waist-High Lob Serve.*

The **WIDE-ANGLE LOB** serve is a combination of the high lob and Z-lob serves. It is designed to finish 39' deep at the center of the back wall. This serve should not carom off the back wall; it was designed to test the receiver's accuracy at placing a ceiling ball. Should the ceiling return not carry correctly into a back corner, you should have an easy setup. (Diagram 3-8 shows the trajectory of the wide-angle lob serve.) The serve hits the front wall 16' to 18' high, and the side wall 18' to 20'. The carom from the front wall then carries the ball to the center of back court about 39' deep.

The final serve in the lob series is the **WAIST-HIGH LOB** serve. Similar to the half lob, it finishes 38' deep and within 6" of the side wall. The important difference is the 6' contact point on the front wall gives you a flat serve. This serve occurs quicker than other lob serves and requires a lightning reaction and a split-second decision on the receiver's part! Occasionally, on the second serve, the receiver will relax and anticipate a slow lob serve to the backhand. If you use the waist-high lob serve, especially to the forehand corner, you have an effective counter weapon. This serve may also be served with the backhand (see Diagram 3-9).

Table 3-1 shows lob serves from different positions in the service box. They represent serves which should be mastered if you are to have the complete lob service game.

Table 3-1:	Lob Serves from Different Serving Positions									
	Service Box Positions									
	1		**2**		**3**		**4**		**5**	
Half Lob	Y	Y	Y	Y	Y	Y	Y	Y	Y	Y
High Lob	Y	Y	Y	Y	Y	Y	Y	Y	Y	Y
Z-Lob		Y		Y	Y	Y		Y		Y
Z-Lob BH		Y		Y		Y				
Wide-Angle Lob		Y	Y	Y	Y	Y	Y	Y		Y
Waist-High Lob		Y	Y	Y	Y	Y	Y	Y	Y	Y
Waist-High Lob BH				Y		Y		Y		
	*FH BH		FH BH		FH BH		FH BH		FH BH	

y = yes, BH = backhand, FH = forehand
*FH BH is the side of the court the ball is served to by the hand of the server.

SERVE SELECTION

The following list is a recommended selection of lob serves against a right-handed opponent who likes to wait on, and shoot, the serve.

SERVE	POISTION
High lob to backhand	4
Waist high lob to backhand (short)	2
Z-lob to backhand (2nd serve)	1
Half lob to backhand	2
Wide-angle lob to backhand	3
High lob to backhand (ceiling)	4
Z-lob to forehand (2nd serve)	3
Half lob to backhand	3
Waist-high lob to forehand	3
Wide-angle lob to backhand	3
Backhand half lob to backhand	4
Backhand Z-lob to backhand	4

By this time you should be convinced if not excited about the prospects of using a lob serve game as an offensive strategy. All that is required of you is practice to develop a good stroke and the variety you need for success. However, the best way to perfect your skill is under game conditions; practice with a partner, each of you serving a specific serving game and each practicing specific returns. The following chapter will introduce another high service game. It will require both power and finesse and should not be attempted until the lob serve game is mastered.

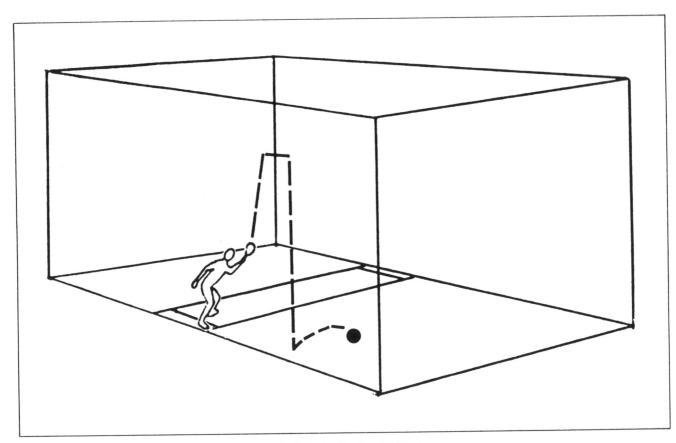

Path of the Overhead Z-Serve.

CHAPTER 4

THE OVERHEAD Z-SERVE

A popular commercial claims that if you do one thing well, success will come your way. When I began working at the University of Pittsburgh, I had been playing racquetball for two years. At Pitt I met fellow racquetball player, Herb Meyers. Herb beat me four days a week, 48 weeks a year for three years. With little more than a unique service game and the brains to make it work, Herb Meyers became 1976 Eastern Regional Doubles Champion.

The champion's unknown service game was the overhead Z-serve. The serve is derived from the overhead tennis serve. Today it is used primarily in racquetball doubles. With a little practice you can succeed, but not just in doubles! These serves can be a great asset to your singles game.

I gradually began to use this service game for my singles matches, and pleasantly I discovered that many players were unable to handle it. This has resulted in numerous victories for me during the last few years.

Marc Auerbach, 1982, suggests that the soft Z-serve is probably the second most frequently used serve, following the drive serve. This serve enters the back court after touching the side wall and crosses the court diagonally, making perception, timing, and setting up for a straight shot difficult for your opponent. The receiver will have few, if any, offensive opportunities when your game is on.

Prior to adding the overhead Z into your game plan, you should understand "why" this serve works! Try to direct the action with your serve to accomplish your goals! It is important to realize that the overhead Z, (particularly the soft and medium speed Z's) will not often result in an ace. The primary purpose of this serve is to: a) get yourself a setup, b) slow your opponents' offensive game down and/or throw it off balance.

ADVANTAGES OF THE OVERHEAD Z-SERVE

1. Keeps your opponent deep in the backhand corner.
2. It is easy for you to keep this serve off the back wall.
3. You can neutralize your opponent's power.
4. The Overhead Z-serve gives you more variety than any other service game possible.
5. You gain a variety of serving angles, and you can alter both height and speed.
6. You can force your opponent to play the ball on the way up or down.
7. The Overhead Z-serve keeps your opponent from settling into a comfortable groove.
8. It gives you an excellent change-of-pace serve.
9. You can exploit the receivers' natural weaknesses, such as backhand shots above the waist.
10. Makes them play **"YOUR"** game!
11. The difficult crossing angles make the ball hard to setup against.

DISADVANTAGES OF THE OVERHEAD Z-SERVE

1. This service game is **NOT** as effective against a **WELL-CONTROLLED DEFENSIVE GAME.** You will not generate setups, and you should switch to the drive serve from time-to-time.
2. Your serve is easily telegraphed because of your court position and the overhand form.

TYPES OF OVERHEAD Z-SERVES INCLUDE:

1. Overhead Z-lob serve.
2. Medium speed overhead Z-serve.
3. Hard drive overhead Z-serve.

THE OVERHEAD Z-LOB SERVE

The overhead Z-lob serve closely resembles the Z-lob serve. It should hit a target on the front wall 16' high and 1' away from the side wall crack. The ball should bounce in the 5' zone and carry high into the backhand corner (39') without touching the walls (see Diagrams 4-1 & 4-2a).

Assume that your opponent is right-handed, and that you are serving to their back-

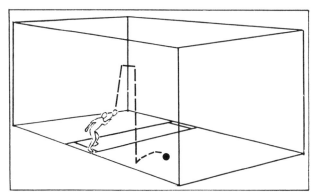

Diagram 4-1. *Path of the Overhead Z-Lob Serve.*

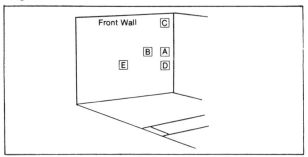

Diagram 4-2A. *Overhead Z-Lob Serve Target.*
B. *Wide Angle Overhead Z-Lob Serve Target.*
C. *Higher-Tighter Overhead Z-Lob Serve Target.*
D. *Hard Drive Overhead Z-Serve Target.*
E. *Hard Overhead Drive Serve Target Straight Into Opposite Corner.*

Photo 4-1. *Face Right Front-Side Wall, Racquet and Ball Shoulder Height.*

hand corner. The position and form I recommend is shown in Pictures 4-1 to 4-5 and described as follows:

1. Stand in the front left corner of the service box facing the right front side wall (see Picture 4-1).
2. If the forehand grip is awkward, use a flat or frying pan grip on the racquet.
3. Hold the racquet at shoulder height in front of your eyes.
4. Bounce the ball directly in front of the racquet so that it bounces at least 2' above your head and hit it on the way up at a point 2' above your head (see Picture 4-2).
5. If the bounce is bad, catch the ball and try it again.
6. Follow-up on the ball with the head of the racquet.
7. When the ball is lined up with your eye, the racquet, and the target, step toward the target and tap the ball lightly toward the front wall (see Pictures 4-3 & 4-4).
8. After serving the ball, pause momentarily to allow the ball to pass the short line. If you move towards center court before the ball crosses the short line you will commit a fault! **"RELAX SLIGHTLY"** (see Picture 4-5).
9. Follow the ball after it passes the short line and drop quickly into the center court position (approximately 27').

Photo 4-2. *Position and Form.*

28

Photo 4-3. *Tap the Ball Lightly.*

Photo 4-5. *Drop Back to Center Court and Relax.*

ADDITIONAL OVERHEAD Z-LOB SERVES

1. Practice serving a wide angle overhead Z-serve, 16' high and 4' away from the side wall corner (see Diagram 4-2b).
2. Next try a higher-tighter serve, 18' by 1' (see Diagram 4-2c).
3. Slice the face of the ball 16' high and 1' wide. The ball should drop down and back after hitting the backhand side wall (see Diagram 4-2a).
4. Practice all serves from the opposite side of the court.

These serves are an excellent weapon against an opponent who expects your lob serve. The only zone from which the receiver can successfully return the serve is small and shoulder high. The receiver has three options within this small zone:

1. Cut the ball off (midair or short hop) and go down-the-line or crosscourt.
2. Hit a ceiling shot before or after the ball strikes the side wall.
3. Attempt a kill or pass shot after the ball drops from the side wall.

The overhead Z-lob serve is very good strategy against a power player, because he/she must return the ball with a high backhand

Photo 4-4. *Follow Through High to Front Wall Target.*

swing. Your opponent must play your serve out of midair, or deep in the backhand corner off the side wall. The shooter must be made to play the midair serve! The defensive player will be forced to play the ball after it hits the side wall.

Consistent winners from these shots are challenging for even a professional player. The receiver who returns every serve at high speed may lose points to the soft, overhead Z. Watch your opponent in case he/she decides to short hop, or cut the ball off in midair. If you are in center court position and the return is poor, you should hopefully be able to end the rally by the third shot.

ADD POWER TO CONTROL THE OPPONENT

The medium power overhead Z-serve is the best serve to use against a new opponent. It will give you valuable information on your opponent's style of play. How does he/she attack the ball and play it out of midair-defensively to the ceiling or offensively with a kill shot?

Secondly, how well does he/she execute their return? Does the return give you a setup, place you in a defensive posture, or effect a side out? Thirdly, how does your opponent let the ball carry off the side wall, Does he/she attempt to play the return? If so, you've got him!

The grip and stance for the overhead Z-serve is the same as for the overhead Z-lob. This stroke uses a full and firm arm swing. The medium power overhead Z should be bounced 8' to 10' high. On the way down, at 7', shoot the ball with full arm extension straight into the target. Then take one step forward, break your wrist, and follow through with your arm swing. Remember, do not hit the ball at an upward or downward angle. **"HIT IT STRAIGHT!"** (see Picture 4-6). The racquet motion is similar to the overarm throw in baseball. The ball should hit the front wall 1' away from the side wall and 7' high. The ball should bounce within the 5' zone past the short line and carom into center court, deep toward the back wall. Because this serve travels faster into back court, the drop after the serve should be faster. Poise yourself for a low return, and keep your racquet low (see Picture 4-7).

Photo 4-6.   *Shoot the Ball Straight to Front Wall.*

Photo 4-7.   *Poise Yourself for a Low Return.*

30

ADD DECEPTION AND VERSATILITY TO THE SERVICE GAME

The hard drive overhead Z-serve is the best tool I know to overcome the disadvantage of telegraphing your serve. This serve is smacked the same way as the medium overhead Z (7' high) except give it more power! The ball should leave the racquet face at a slight downward angle toward the front wall target, 5' to 6' high and 1' away from the side wall (see Diagram 4-2d).

The ball should shoot down past the short line, with the bounce hitting the side wall and continuing upwards toward the back wall. This serve should keep your opponent deep in the backcourt and allow you a variety of serves. You will throw their timing off! Remember to drop quickly back into center court. Assess your opponent, react quickly, and take the offensive shot!

SERVING STRATEGY

Think of the overhead Z-service and imagine that you are a baseball pitcher. You now have a six-serve repertoire to both sides of the court. How many major league pitchers can boast six pitches? The following strategy discusses when and why to use each type of serve.

The medium power overhead Z-serve will keep your opponent in the back court. This serve is very difficult to effectively cut off in midair because it is fast! Bounce the ball 7' to 8' high in the service box, then shoot it straight to the front wall target. Do not hit the ball upward at an angle, or strike it too hard. You want to draw the receiver in so he/she has to play the ball out of midair. After he/she has run in, give him/her a hard driving overhead Z-serve. You can catch him/her running in and jam the return any time you want.

Next, give him/her a high overhead Z-lob serve. You should catch them waiting on the serve this time, which forces him/her to return deep. Next, try your forehand side and repeat the same three serve series. Your opponent should be dizzy by now.

Remember, vary the height, spin, angle, and power on each and every serve. Use the overhead serving technique with the hard overhead drive straight into the opposite corner for even more variety (see Diagrams 4-2e & 4-3).

Watch your opponent from the corner of your eye prior to serving. The receiver may move to the left side wall too soon! Then you will have him/her in your pocket. Here is a serving strategy list:

SERVING STRATEGIES
1. Medium power overhead Z
2. Hard overhead Z
3. Soft overhead Z
4. Hard overhead Z
5. Hard overhead drive
6. Medium overhead Z
7. Wide angle, overhead Z-lob
8. Slice overhead Z-lob
9. Hard overhead Z
10. Extra-high, overhead Z-lob

Remember that in these situations you are in the center court and you control the match. **"THINK OFFENSE!"** Do not give up your edge with a defensive third shot. If the opponent attempts to kill the ball you should have an easy time covering the shot. Around-the-wall balls should be cut off in midair. You can shoot them into the corners or down-the-line. Pass shots should be pinched into the front court.

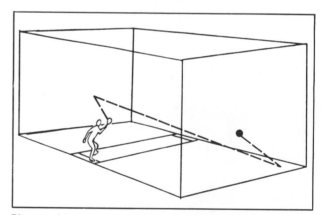

Diagram 4-3. *Path of Hard Overhead Drive Serve.*

LOOK FOR THESE COMMON ERRORS

The most common error for many players is striking the side wall first, thereby losing the serve. All teachers should check their student's grip, body position relative to the corner, and their step into the shot. Their ball should not hit the front wall too far to the left, or too hard! If it does, it will then strike the right side wall too far back and travel into the center of the back court. The receiver will have a back wall setup in that case.

Some students may have difficulty stroking the ball correctly. First, have them stand 30' from the front wall and practice throwing the ball straight to the front wall with an overarm motion. Second, position them in the service box as if they were going to serve and have them throw the ball with the same arm motion at the overhead Z targets.

Another common error is remaining too close to the side wall after the serve. This gives the receiver most of the court for the return. You must always move quickly to the deep center court position to remain in command. This setup position will prevent you from being hit with the return, and will increase your chances for a rekill.

If I haven't convinced you, by now, that the overhead Z-service game will win matches, remember that I learned this service game from a regional champ, Herb Meyers. I practiced this serve until I just couldn't get any better. One year later, we met as opponents in a tournament situation; my strategy was simple, to use the overhead Z-service game and win! I lost the match, and I later asked Herb what I had done wrong. "Nothing," he retorted, "You have just received a lesson on how to neutralize the overhead Z-service game."

Feet Staggered and Touching Short Line. Hands Aligned With Sweet Spot of Racquetball.

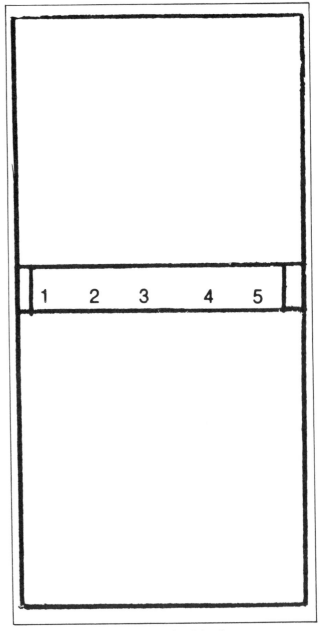

Start Positions for Drive Serve.

CHAPTER 5

REVIEW OF SERVING FUNDAMENTALS

The serve in racquetball may be easily compared to the pitch in baseball since both actions are executed in an attempt to exploit an opponent's weakness. When you serve, you have a distinct advantage over your opponent — don't give your advantage up by letting your opponent have a second shot. **"BEAT THEM ON THE SERVE!"** An analytical approach to the service game is a valuable weapon, and should be a major part of your mental game. There are five basic serves (Drive, Z, Jam, Lob, and Overhead Z); varying height, direction, speed, spins, and starting position provide an infinite number of workable combinations.

GOOD SERVING FORM:

1. Practice your serves alone and before the match.
2. Develop a variety of serves from the same starting position.
3. Use the same smooth and consistent swing for every serve.
4. Step toward the target on the front wall at the beginning of the serve.
5. Watch your serve past the short line, setup for center court control, look at the opponent to anticipate the type of return, then move into position to be ahead of the return.
6. If your opponent attempts to kill on every return of serve, move closer to front wall and wait to rekill the return.
7. If you serve to your backhand side, rotate your grip on the follow-through and expect a backhand return.
8. If you serve to the forehand side, maintain your forehand grip and be ready.
9. Slide into the V position, behind short line, and setup for next shot (see Diagram 5-1).

BASIC SERVING STRATEGY

1. Never change a successful service game.
2. Always change a losing serving game.

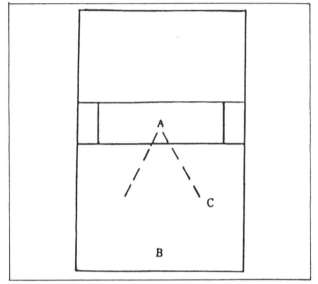

Diagram 5-1. *V Position Behind Short Line, Setup for Next Shot.*

3. It often happens that both opponents have returned each others' serves consistently and the score remains tied for several serve changes. Recognize this situation and alter your serving pattern immediately.
   a. Change drive serves to high soft lobs.
   b. Vary high hard Z's with low short drives.
   c. Switch serve from backhand to forehand.
4. Never serve the same serve twice in a row.
5. Never serve the same second serve twice in a row.
6. Force your opponent to return your serve on the run; this makes the return harder for him/her.
7. Keep your serves off the back wall (except the Jam).
8. Use deception in your service motion.

PREPARING FOR A MATCH

Upon entering a match against a new opponent, you should plan an offensive serving strategy similar to that of a quarterback in football or a pitcher in baseball. Find your opponent's weaknesses in returning serves, this is critical toward winning the match! Your first six to twelve serves should be a mixture of several types, speeds, and placements of the ball (shallow or deep, left or right). Place your opponent's returns into three categories; (1) serves returned offensively; (2) serves returned defensively, and (3) ace serves or serves returned for a setup. Now you should employ those serves which were unreturnable by your opponent. If your opponent handles all of your serves, choose serves which generate desired returns for you to cover. Your game plan should be flexible. **"THINK!"**

The following concepts and specifics about the serve will broaden your understanding of the game. Look at the court in Diagram 5-2. The dotted areas labeled A represent the near service corners. The dotted areas labeled B represent the far service corners. Understanding this will increase the finesse of your serving game.

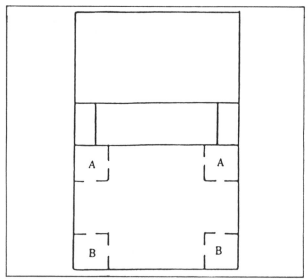

Diagram 5-2. *The four corners of the service zone.*

1. At service is the best time to control the pace of the game. Take your time, relax, think through the serve mentally prior to serving. Visualize (mental imagery) the serve to the front wall target and follow it onto the back court. Watch the serve crack out.
2. Look at the receiver before the serve to see if the receiver is out of position.
3. Many racquetball players return serves better with their backhand. Do not be afraid to serve to an opponent's forehand.
4. If your opponent leans toward the backhand, serve a drive to the forehand.
5. If your opponent is short, serve high lobs and high Z-lobs.

6. If your opponent is tall, serve drives, jams, and low Z serves.
7. If your opponent sets up close to the rear wall, serve to the front corners of the service court (see Diagram 5-2, label A).
8. If your opponent sets up close to the front of the service area, drive serves or high lobs to the back service boxes will send him/her running (see Diagram 5-2, Label B).
9. Some players use extra long racquets, supposedly for more power and greater reach. In reality, the extra racquet length may be cumbersome in back corners and near the side walls. Serve Z's or lobs close to the side wall to check your opponent's racquet control.
10. When, occasionally, a large-slow opponent can't get out of his/her own way, serve a Jam serve directly at his/her body.
11. Force a tired opponent to run to return your serve. Even consider wasting your first serve (long) to make your opponent expend more energy.
12. If you're playing an ex-tennis player, go with hard Z serves to both forehand and backhand.
13. If your opponent waits on a high lob serve, repeat frequently, add spins and keep the serve off the back wall.

Practice makes perfect! Remember this true cliche. If you make the effort to perfect your serve, you will be rewarded with many victories. Your serve initiates all play, and it keeps your opponent off balance. A well-thought-out serve will destroy any opponent's mental game. The mental game is half of the game. Each serve (Low-Z, High-Z, Lob, Short Drive, Long Drive) should be practiced separately to both forehand and backhand sides of the court.

Practice serving from all five positions in the service box. This provides easy access to center court control and a balanced retrieving position for your opponent's return. As you master each serve, experiment with spins and speeds, while observing the effects.

Practice setting up in center court, and gain control after each serve. A serve which throws you off balance and prevents you from moving into a good retrieving position is a bad serve. Drop it! After setting up for the return, practice running to all four corners and both sides of the court, these star or four-corner drills are excellent conditioners which will extend your coverage of the court. Good luck and may you have many aces.

CHAPTER 6

MIDDLE COURT PLAY — WHERE THE GAME IS WON OR LOST!

The opportunity to utilize the middle (mid) court is always present in racquetball. Take advantage of this situation! Two-thirds of all shots can be retrieved from midcourt. Make good midcourt play your mission. The midcourt area is the service line (15ft.) to 30ft. from the front wall (see Diagram 6-1).

Every shot hit from midcourt is controlled by you and your opponents' positions. For example, a forehand shot to the right front court with your opponent in the middle of the service area (or forward) is best returned with a down-the-line pass on the right side. Diagram 6-1 illustrates the different strategy areas of the racquetball court.

Do not confuse midcourt with center court; center court is an area within midcourt (see Diagram 6-1). Both areas dictate special shot strategies. Both have definite characteristics which can contribute to your winning matches in racquetball. For greater court coverage, run towards center court after hitting your shot. Midcourt is where the majority of any game will be played.

Many players are stronger in the back court than in midcourt. Whether your strength is in midcourt or back court, spend as much time as possible in center court. If you can control center court by keeping your opponent trapped in the back court, you will control the match. From midcourt, a player is also able to take any shot with an excellent chance of a kill. Retrieve your opponent's next shot; it will be only a few steps away if you can get to a good center court position.

Center court play requires aggressiveness. Take advantage of your position by playing the ball offensively; move laterally to cut off passes. Advance quickly to the front court to dispose of any missed kill shot attempts by your opponent. Always move toward center court immediately after a shot unless you anticipate another shot in another area. Hesitation could mean a lost opportunity. Move after **YOUR** shot, not your opponent's.

This section should provide beginners with a basic understanding of the value of good midcourt play. The next section will discuss the value of practice from center court.

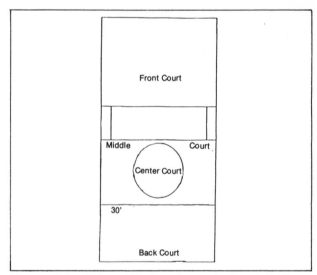

Diagram 6-1. *Different Strategy Areas of a Racquetball Court.*

BEGINNERS — PRACTICE TO WIN

Plan to work one hour a week to structured practice on the racquetball court. Practice is essential to improving every aspect of your game, and also to iron out common errors. Practice will improve both your self-confidence and concentration.

Divide the court into six areas which approximate where most shots occur. Practice from the six positions as identified in Diagram 6-2. Try to attain an 80% success rate before moving to intermediate techniques. This same ratio of success also applies to intermediate players. Don't move ahead before you are ready. Be honest with yourself.

WARNING! Practicing at more difficult skill levels will be wasted without proper stroke mechanics and consistency. Your flaws will be negatively reinforced!

Positions #1 through #5 in Diagram 6-2 offer a variety of shot selections to practice. These shots include most types of passes, kills, and pass/kills from both forehand and backhand sides. During play, 80-90% of all shots will come from these positions. Position #6 is used to practice specific midcourt drills in a confined area. During actual play, the shot situations occur in midcourt.

Position #3 is better defined as an area, since center court varies with style of play, shots hit, the ball, court walls, and the opponent. Center court practice drills are recommended from the four positions in Area 3. This chapter describes in detail the drills to be practiced from these positions.

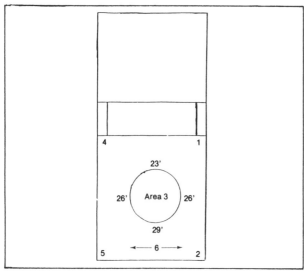

Diagram 6-2. *Six Practice Positions.*

INTERMEDIATE PLAYERS — CUT THE BALL OFF

Aggressive play (cutting the ball off) will give your game an added lift in several important ways. First, you'll score the easy points by maintaining your position in the center court area.

Secondly, by keeping a toehold in center court and holding your position, you will be dictating the action. This ploy will keep your opponent constantly on the defensive and reduce his/her game and draw many weak returns.

Third, cutting the ball off will create a variety of scoring options if your opponent is off balance or out of position. Be quick; angle

the ball away before your opponent recovers. Use your body position to legally block him/her as you snap the ball into the open court.

Fourth, your opponent's offensive attempt may be left up and come hard through midcourt. You must know how and when to cut this shot off in the air or after one bounce. The ball also can be played off the back wall. Often, though, you are well-advised to intercept the ball. Take it low and try to score. Use the straight-in kill, a tight pinch, or a pass. You will still have good court position to cover the next shot.

ADVANCED PLAYERS — DEVELOP A MIDCOURT STANCE

Your objective in midcourt should be to use an efficient upper body swing which will minimize the number of setups for your opponent. Your upper body and hips should move freely through the shot regardless of foot position. The following checklist offers guidelines on ideal body technique.

CHECKLIST FOR OPEN STANCE
1. Face the front wall (see Picture 6-1).
2. Expand your hitting base - feet wide apart.
3. Bend your knees.
4. Do not step into the ball. Hold your ground and use a fencer's lunge or crossover step (see Pictures 6-2 & 6-3).
5. Carry your racquet at mid-thigh.
6. Rotate your hips as much as possible.
7. Rotate your shoulders as in full stroke (whipping action (see Pictures 6-4 & 6-5).
8. The down angle of your arm and racquet swing should be greater than normal (see Pictures 6-6 & 6-7).
9. Snap your wrist in the contact zone (firm wrist cock) (see Picture 6-8).
10. Contact all balls at waist level and below (see Picture 6-9).
11. Use a full, but compact, follow-through (see Picture 6-10).
12. Direction and accuracy are more important than power.
13. Master the pinch, pass, straight kill, reverse pinch, and fly kill.
14. Master all shots from the four center court positions shown in Diagram 6-2.

HITTING ON THE RUN

Some players think that anything they hit on the run should be flipped back to the front wall to maintain the rally. However, you will lose scoring opportunities by giving the

Photo 6-1. *Face Front Wall.*

Photo 6-3. *Crossover Step. (greater range, less balance)*

Photo 6-2. *Fencer's Lunge. (shorter range, better balance)*

Photo 6-4. *Arm Swing to Begin Whipping Action.*

Photo 6-5. *Rotate Shoulder Back.*

Photo 6-7. *Wrist Cocked.*

Photo 6-6. *Down Swing.*

Photo 6-8. *Snap Wrist Through Contact Zone.*

Photo 6-9. *Contact Ball at or Below Wrist Level.*

Photo 6-10. *Compact Follow-Through.*

opponent floaters to kill. Many top players cannot hit kill shots on the run. They have, however, the ability to hit good passing shots or the sense to go to the ceiling when they are out of position or in trouble.

When the ball is away from your body, you will be forced to stretch wide or to hit while on the run. You must learn to convert these shots to winners. A good player can shoot a setup, while a great player can hit the ball effectively on the run. Although we often have to play the ball on the run, few players actually practice this situation. First, practice the form shown in Pictures 6-4 to 6-10. These leg movements will make your retrieval both efficient and accurate. The stroke is finished with the extension of your arm and the snap of your wrist. Second, hit yourself easy setups which will enable you to move as if you were playing. Third, practice the Blind Reaction Drill and the Kill and Close Drill described later in Chapter Eight. Remember, stepping into the ball and using good form should be in the back of your mind as you retrieve the ball. When the ball is moving at 50 to 80 mph, accuracy is what counts most!

DRILLS FOR ALL LEVELS OF PLAY

ALLEY DRILL

The alley drill is the fundamental drill in racquetball. All players use this drill, consciously or not, when warming up. Correct and purposefull drill performance, however, is often overlooked. This drill was named for an imaginary line which extends from the doubles line in the service box and runs the length of the court.

The player stands at Position 1, approximately 6" outside the line, facing the side wall. Drop the ball inside the line, allow one bounce, and stroke to the front wall. When hit correctly, the ball should go straight to the front wall, travel straight back down the alley (6" to 18" high), and pass between the side wall and the player without touching the wall (see Diagram 6-3).

The **BEGINNER** should use this drill to develop basic forehand and backhand strokes and spacial awareness between the body, the racquet, and the wall. A feeling for the contact point will develop while watching the racquet hit the ball. The **INTERMEDIATE PLAYER** should perform the alley drill without a bounce, dropping the ball and hitting before it reaches the floor. This variation will shorten and quicken the swing, generate more power, and develop lower shots. The **ADVANCED PLAYER** should be able to rally the ball continuously while maintaining complete control over the ball, by making subtle stroke changes, and developing better footwork.

39

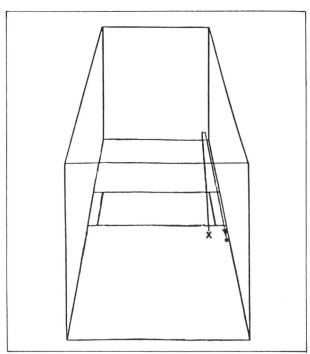

Diagram 6-3. *The Alley Drill.*

The **TEACHING-PRO** will use the drill to teach beginners and to correct their students' bad habits. If you hit the ball at the proper contact point, it will travel straight to and from the front wall. If the ball hits the side wall going to the front wall, the contact point was too deep in your stance. If the ball travels away from the body and angles cross court, the contact point was too far ahead of your body. Make sure that the students know why their shots are going off line. If the student swings with a stiff wrist resembling a tennis stroke, move the student towards the side wall and repeat the drill. This technique will force the student to keep elbows in, bringing the arm swing down, and snapping the wrist upon contact. An exaggerated backswing can be corrected if you place the student in the correct form at Position #2 with the racquet on the back wall; this action will force the student to bring the racquet forward. Remedy an unusual hitch by hitting the ball without a bounce. This quicker swing does not allow time for a hitch to develop. Use the alley drill from any position along the side walls to practice specific shot situations including pinch, splat, and crosscourt.

WRIST DROP

The wrist drop drill is as important to your racquetball game as brushing your teeth is to your personal hygiene. Because it is difficult, most players overlook this drill; having the benefits from mastery of the drill are enormous. It will improve your back wall play, retrieval ability, and midcourt success.

First, face the right side wall with your racquet in front of your body. Use the forehand grip with the front face of the racquet turned up so the ball will balance on left center of the racquet (see Picture 6-11). Drop your racquet from under the ball, turn the racquet sideways cocking the wrist simultaneously, and snap the wrist forward **HITTING THE BALL BEFORE IT REACHES THE FLOOR** (see Pictures 6-12 to 6-14). Keep your eyes on the ball. Relax, and be patient. In time, you will be successful.

The **BEGINNER** should start with the racquet held waist-high. Practice your swing without the ball until you achieve the correct motion. Standing 10 ft. from the front wall, balance the ball on the racquet, and pause before shooting it. This drill should be considered a success if the ball hits the front wall. The beginner will not be able to execute the backhand wrist drop.

The **INTERMEDIATE PLAYER** should begin 20 ft. from the front wall. The racquet will be a mid-thigh level. Experienced players should be able to perform the backhand wrist

Photo 6-11. *Balance Ball Left of Center.*

40

Photo 6-12. *Drop the Racquet.*

Photo 6-14. *Snap Wrist, Hit Ball Before it Reaches Floor.*

Photo 6-13. *Turn Racquet, Cocking Wrist.*

drop by moving closer to the front wall. Hold the **BACK FACE** of the racquet turned up so the ball will balance on the right center of the racquet (see Picture 6-15). The remainder of the drill is the same as the forehand (see Pictures 6-16 to 6-18). The **ADVANCED PLAYER** should practice 30 ft. to 38 ft. from the front wall with the racquet at knee level.

The **TEACHING-PRO** will use the drill to develop correct wrist-snapping motion, strength in the forearm muscles, and lightning-fast reflexes. **NOTE,** students should try to avoid the common error of lifting the ball with the racquet before the drill starts.

RALLY AND VOLLEY REDIRECT DRILLS

The rally and volley redirect drills are a series of drills which increase in difficulty at all skill levels. Their purpose is to improve your midcourt game, footwork, and your ability to put the ball away. These drills are more easily mastered from Position #6 toward the side wall by redirecting the ball into the back wall corners. Practicing in a small area will aid your efforts, even though the game situation will occur in midcourt while facing the front wall.

Photo 6-15. *Backface of Racquet Turned Up.*

Photo 6-17. *Turn Racquet, Cocking Wrist.*

Photo 6-16. *Drop the Racquet.*

Photo 6-18. *Snap Wrist, Hit Ball Before it Reaches Floor.*

The form for all drills is the same. Face the side wall crouched low. Place your racquet in front of your body. Keep on your toes with your feet about shoulder-width apart. Then move behind the ball to play the shot (see Diagram 6-4).

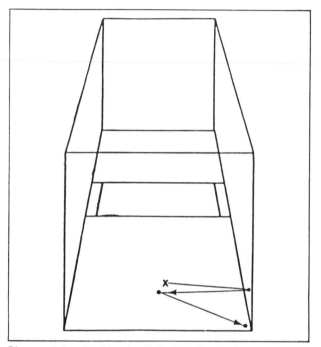

Diagram 6-4. *Position for Rally & Volley Redirect Drills.*

In this first drill for **BEGINNERS,** play the ball into the side wall twice on a bounce with the forehand. On your third shot, redirect the shot into the back wall corner with a short, firm stroke. Repeat this stroke until you have developed a rhythm and successfully controlled the ball. The second drill is for you to turn around, face the other side wall, and repeat the process with the backhand.

INTERMEDIATE PLAYERS can increase this drill's difficulty by rallying the ball forehand to backhand and back-to forehand for the redirection into the corner. Repeat on the opposite side of the court for the backhand. **ADVANCED PLAYERS** should **VOLLEY** (midair) the ball into the wall twice with the forehand. Fly kill the ball, forehand or backhand, into the corner to build your confidence. Repeat this drill in the opposite direction with both forehand to backhand and a backhand fly kill into the corner.

TEACHING-PROS should use the speed of the ball and the height of the ball from the side wall to increase difficulty. Strive continually for harder and lower shots. Common mistakes for the student include: reaching too far

in front of the body for the ball rather than waiting; improper setup with the first two shots; and, overpowering the redirected shot.

DROP CORNER AND CROSSCORNER KILL DRILLS

These drills will also become progressively difficult. Every player should master each skill level before advancing. All of the drills should be practiced from each of the four positions in Area 3 with an open stance while facing the front wall (see Diagram 6-2 & 6-5).

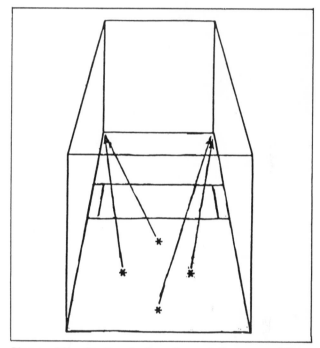

Diagram 6-5. *Position for Drop Corner & Crosscourt Kill Drills.*

BEGINNERS start at 23 ft., drop the ball, allow one bounce, then shoot the ball into the corner. Repeat the drill with the forehand to the forehand corner; then the forehand to the backhand corner. The backhand should be similarly practiced. The drills must be practiced from all four positions in Area #3. **INTERMEDIATE PLAYERS** should perform this drill without a bounce, concentrating on form. Allow the ball to drop low enough for a kill shot. **ADVANCED PLAYERS** can complete these drills by rallying the ball from a front wall setup. Remember, to practice all shot combinations while you continuously kill and rekill the ball.

TEACHING-PROS should emphasize the open stance form. Pay close attention to your student's hip and shoulder rotation through the shot. The most common mistake is to use just arm swing to hit the ball; another mistake is the flat or horizontal arm swing. The ball then stays up and is retrieved easily by your opponent. The arm swing should be aimed down toward the bottom board.

FRONT SIDE WALL SETUP DRILL

The first six months of learning to play racquetball will involve mastering the geometry of the game; this drill will accelerate the process. **BEGINNERS** should face the front wall. Hit a setup off the front side wall. Allow the ball one bounce. Turn your body sideways with the racquet back and then hit a down-the-line shot. Make sure to adjust your body to face the side wall. **INTERMEDIATE PLAYERS** should repeat the procedure with more emphasis on killing the ball in the corners. **ADVANCED PLAYERS** should practice killing the ball cross-corner (see Diagram 6-6).

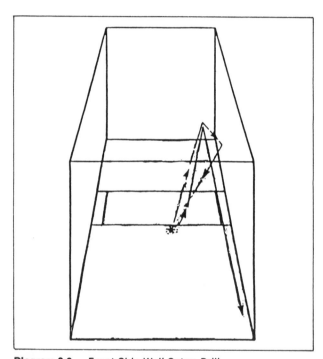

Diagram 6-6. *Front Side Wall Setup Drill.*

TEACHING-PROS should be aware that beginners will have more difficulty in learning to setup the ball, than in executing their actual shots. Setup the ball for them. Some common errors include planting the feet too soon, and reaching in front of the body to play the ball. This is usually the result of not having the racquet back soon enough into the ready position. Learning to hit setups at the contact point is also a common problem. The proper setup will enable the student to swing correctly, hit the ball, and move forward through the contact point (keep the feet moving).

VOLLEY OR FLY DRILLS

The ability to play shots from midair is often the difference between the **ADVANCED PLAYER** and the **CHAMPION**. Volley shot practice from center court is essential for the advanced player. Hit a hard shot 4 ft high into the front wall. Play the return out of midair; down-the-line, near corner, and crosscorner. The ball may hit the side wall or front wall first. Do not reach for the ball. Hold your ground, and wait. Practice the fencer's lunge and crossover step to see which works best (see Diagram 6-7).

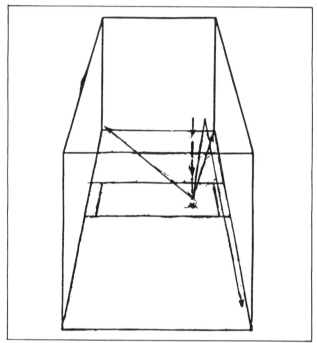

Diagram 6-7. *Volley and Fly Kill Drills.*

BACK WALL TO FRONT WALL VOLLEY KILL

The back-to-front wall volley kill is another game situation drill. The situation occurs when the opponent cannot get the racquet behind the ball for a normal return; i.e., Z-serve or the opponent is passed and, in desperation, keeps the ball in play by hitting it into the back wall.

BEGINNER and **INTERMEDIATE PLAYERS** tend to let the ball bounce off the front wall into the back court. Your opponent will then have time to recover to center court position. An **ADVANCED PLAYER** will not give the opponent the opportunity to recover. The advanced player will volley-kill the ball from midair into the front corners.

BEGINNERS should practice this drill with a partner. Have your partner stand in the back court and hit the ball off the back wall. Then position yourself in center court and watch the ball. You should move forward to play the shot from midair as it comes off the front wall. The advantage for the beginning player will come from watching the ball, and learning which angles the ball can take off the walls (see Diagram 6-8).

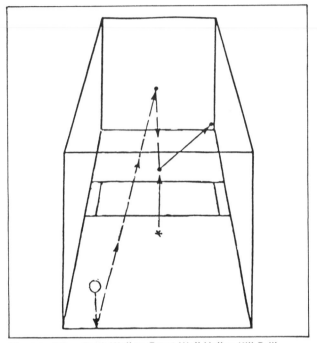

Diagram 6-8. *Back Wall to Front Wall Volley Kill Drill.*

INTERMEDIATE PLAYERS can practice this drill in a similar way, but will not watch the ball. They will listen for the sound coming off the back wall and pick it up overhead. Concentrate on letting the ball drop low off the front wall before hitting the kill shot into the corners. **ADVANCED PLAYERS** should use this drill for practice and as a conditioner. Have the balls hit faster off the back wall. Use two helpers to hit balls one after another, alternating sides. This drill will keep the advanced players scrambling in and out of center court.

TEACHING-PROS should notice whether the student overruns the ball. The student might also reach overhead for a shot, hitting the ball downward at an acute angle.

BLIND REACTION DRILL

The blind reaction drill comprehensively includes the benefits of the previous midcourt drills, enabling you to practice midcourt game situations and improve your reflexes. It is also an excellent conditioning exercise which teaches proper footwork.

BEGINNERS should position themselves in center court. Face the front wall with the racquet low in front of your body. The retriever remains poised while the partner stands behind, hitting the ball to the front wall. Your partner should hit the ball so you can reach the ball and return it to the corner for a winner (see Diagram 6-9).

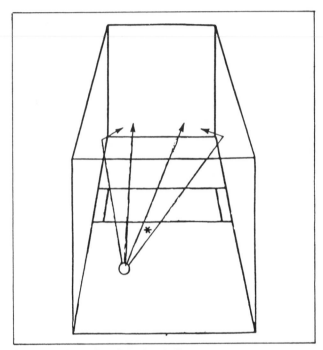

Diagram 6-9. *Blind Reaction Drill.*

INTERMEDIATE PLAYERS can increase this drill's difficulty with the use of greater speed, repetition, and distance to cover the shot. **ADVANCED PLAYERS** can start in the back court and run forward while the partner shoots the ball off the front wall. Retrieve and rekill the ball while on the run.

TEACHING-PROS should emphasize the proper footwork needed to retrieve the ball laterally. Teach the crossover step or fencer's lunge from the beginning. Some common errors include improper arm swing and wrist snap, soft shots overpowering the ball, and not knowing how to play the ball.

MIDDLE COURT SHOT STRATEGY

Drill practice in midcourt is useless without a method. Table 6-1 outlines the percentage shots given your position and that of your opponent. Beginners should master Shot #1 on the chart before trying Shot #2. Intermediates should master the first two shots before attempting Shot #3. Advanced players can use all three shots.

Table 6-1:

Percentage shots given your position and that of your opponent

		YOUR OPPONENT'S POSITION	
		FRONT COURT	**CENTER COURT**
YOUR POSITION WHEN HITTING THE BALL	FRONT COURT	1. Down-the-line pass 2. Crosscourt pass 3. Z-ball	1. Kill down-the-line 2. Pinch shot 3. Reverse pinch shot
	CENTER COURT	1. Down-the-line pass 2. Crosscourt pass 3. Ceiling ball	1. Corner kill shot 2. Reverse kill shot 3. Wide-angle pass

Fencer's Lunge. (better balance)

Crossover Step. (greater range)

CHAPTER 7

IMPROVE YOUR RETURN OF SERVE AND WIN

"I don't care where you serve," says Marty Hogan, "because I'm going to kill everything you serve." Hogan positions himself near the back wall and starts moving forward with the serve to play the serve on the run.

"Boy, am I going to hustle on this play," says Steve Strandemo. Steve is 6 ft. from the back wall, hunched over, with legs spread wide. Strandemo feels he can move faster from a wide, upright stance.

Charlie Brumfield believes the best strategy is to gamble one way or the other. Since 90% of all serves go to the backhand, move to the left a few times. Brumfield will move far to the left before the server even hits the ball. The server will then think twice and you may catch him/her off guard. Brumfield also believes it is better to be aced several times from incorrect guesses than to remain in center court and return none of the serves effectively.

These champion racquetball professionals have developed return of serve strategies which complement their style of play. However, a fundamental premise which many students of racquetball seem to forget is to practice and execute only techniques which are within their physical capabilities. None of these positions perhaps is the best way for you to cover the ball. Only Marty Hogan can get away with his kill method. Steve Strandemo tries to cover the entire court, and Charlie Brumfield attempts to outguess the server. The less experienced player will need to blend these differing styles into one which will be effective and consistent against different servers for themselves.

Remember, the serve is still the most powerful weapon in racquetball today. The advantages of a superior service game outweigh every other racquetball skill in determining who wins. As evidence to support this statement, the experts are continually experimenting with rule modifications which will diminish the advantage of the server. The following changes are being considered; a screen serve is a fault serve, one serve in lieu of

two, reducing the width of the service box to keep the server in the middle, and a suggestion to draw a horizontal line at 25 ft. where the serve must clear, in lieu of the present 20 ft. short line.

In terms of importance, the return of serve is as significant as the serve in determining the outcome of the rally. If the all-powerful serve is where the game of racquetball is won, then the return of serve is where the game is lost.

POSITION, ANTICIPATION, AND CONCENTRATION

To receive the serve, position yourself approximately 4 ft. from the back wall in the center of the court. Do not lean to either side. Stay on your toes, knees slightly bent, in a crouch position. Your racquet should be in front of your body, and you should use a backhand grip with your wrist cocked. Let your body maintain motion by swaying slightly. It is easier to start moving when you sway! Keep your eyes on the ball from the time the server enters the service box. Anticipation, a practiced plan, and you setting up for the return, are most important to remember if you are going to return the serve.

If your opponent crouches low, expect a drive or Z-serve. You should crouch and remain low while moving for the return. If the server stands erect, expect a lob serve. Rise out of your crouch position, and keep your racquet about waist-high. Your first movement should be toward where the ball has been served. Use a crossover step in either direction; this will provide you with a good hitting position when you return the ball. While you crossover, your shoulders should face the back wall. With your wrist cocked, bring your racquet back into the hitting position. You are now ready to hit a solid return.

Off the court, practice this technique. Try to make your mind blank, close your eyes, and imagine the front wall of the court. Locate the ball on the front wall, and gradually move closer towards the ball until you can see the seam. Look past this seam into the texture and crevices of the ball's surface. This technique will improve your length of concentration on the ball.

You might think mental practice techniques would be impossible to use against the first-rate serve. Not true! This technique can become a great advantage to you in tournament play after only several months of experimentation. The more alert you are mentally, the quicker and more accurate your reactions will become against any opponent. This concentration will aid you in slowing down your perception of time, giving you the extra awareness to see and place the ball accurately. By meeting the ball before it hits the side wall, and cutting off the angle from a serve, you gain a great advantage. Reaching center court before the server gains control of this area is very important to the winning game. If either a top-flight amateur or a professional were to perfect this technique, a minor revolution in the game of racquetball would take place. The longstanding advantage of the server would be reversed.

During your practice sessions, try to master specific returns for every serve imaginable. After you have anticipated what serve your opponent is going to hit, mentally select your return, and imagine yourself executing it perfectly.

BEGINNERS: THINK OF CENTER COURT CONTROL

Regardless of your level of play, your return of serve must have thought behind it. The overwhelming factor in winning for levels of play, especially for the beginner, is the achievement and maintenance of center court position (see Diagram 7-1). Whether you accomplish this by a good serve, a well-placed return of serve, or by controlling center court throughout the rally, the player who controls center court will usually win the match.

The receiver is located near the back wall while the server is near center court at the beginning of play. The purpose of the service return is to win the exchange of the serve. The most effective defensive shot is the ceiling ball. As Table 7-1 reveals, a ceiling ball is a high percentage shot even for the beginning player. Almost any serve has a large margin of error allowable, if you hit a decent ceiling ball. After you hit a ceiling ball return, move back into the center court, and watch the server for a clue as to his/her next shot. React accordingly!

Tables 7-1, 7-2, and 7-3 represent the skill levels for club players. The percentages represent the expected rate of success if the shot is executed correctly. This does not mean you will win the rally, it means you will neutralize the serve.

INTERMEDIATE PLAYERS: CONTROL THE RALLY WITH THE RETURN OF SERVE

The intermediate player must develop a minimum of two serve returns for every serve. Determine which returns are more easily mastered and learn those first. Be versatile, but within your personal limitations. Attempt only shots that you have practiced and can execute well in game situations. Referring to Table 7-2, the intermediate player can expect a higher percentage of success from these suggested returns: the ceiling ball, around-the-wall ball, down-the-line pass, and crosscourt passing shot. The shots with the largest margin for errors, shots that have the largest target area and can be hit while moving, standing still, or on and off balance are the shots which will finish the job with minimal calculated risk. Remember, it is vitally important to practice these shots with different serves!

Another suggestion on the return of serve is for you to move up and play the ball offensively on the fly, or short hop as often as possible. Hit the passing shot down-the-line or cross court. These shots can be anywhere from 6" to 3' high, so a perfect shot is unnecessary. You need just enough to draw the opponent out of the middle so you can glide into center court. Do not let the ball trap you to one side or in the back corners.

Remember, hit an aggressive return (pass shot) if the ball can be taken below the

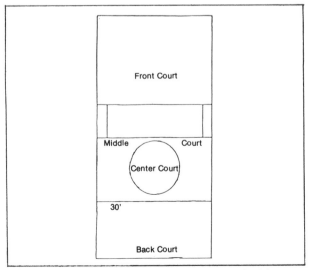

Diagram 7-1. *Gain and Maintain Center Court Position.*

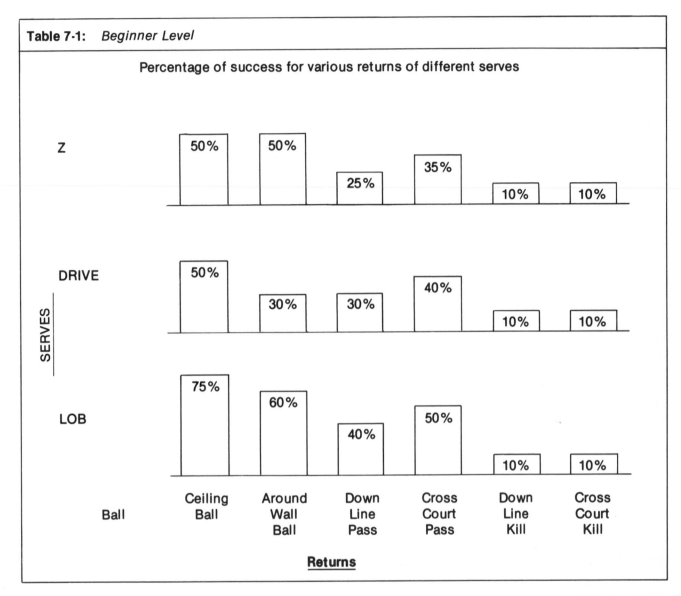

Table 7-1: *Beginner Level*

Percentage of success for various returns of different serves

SERVES	Ceiling Ball	Around Wall Ball	Down Line Pass	Cross Court Pass	Down Line Kill	Cross Court Kill
Z	50%	50%	25%	35%	10%	10%
DRIVE	50%	30%	30%	40%	10%	10%
LOB	75%	60%	40%	50%	10%	10%

Returns

waist. Be aggressive because the pass must be hard enough to get past the server, but not so high that it comes off the back wall. Hit a ceiling ball or an around-the-wall shot if the ball must be taken above the waist. If nothing else seems to be working, employ the Third Law of Racquetball — keep your returns down-the-line.

ADVANCED PLAYERS: END THE RALLY WITH THE RETURN OF SERVE

The advanced player's purpose on the return of serve should be to end the rally without losing points. An advanced player is not necessarily a player who attempts to kill the ball all the time. The advanced player can vary from four to six returns, both offensive and defensive, from any serve. More importantly, the advanced player is wise enough to know his/her limitations.

You should divide your body into hitting zones to learn your specific capabilities. By playing the ball from the knees down, you should be capable of hitting any defensive shot, any passing shot, and a good percentage (50%) of pass/kills. From waist level, defensive balls have a high percentage, passing shots are still a good bet, but the success in kill shot attempts drops. Above chest level, defensive balls have a high percentage, pass shots become mid-to-low percentage, and kill shots become very low percentage. Therefore, you must learn not to beat yourself when trying to control the center court.

Table 7-3 should be further interpreted to reflect the height of the ball the receiver is about to return. Lob and Z-lob serves are chest level serves, Z's and jams are waist level serves, while drives are knee level and below. For example, with the ball in the high contact zone (lob serve), the advanced player can only de-

49

Table 7-2: *Intermediate Level*

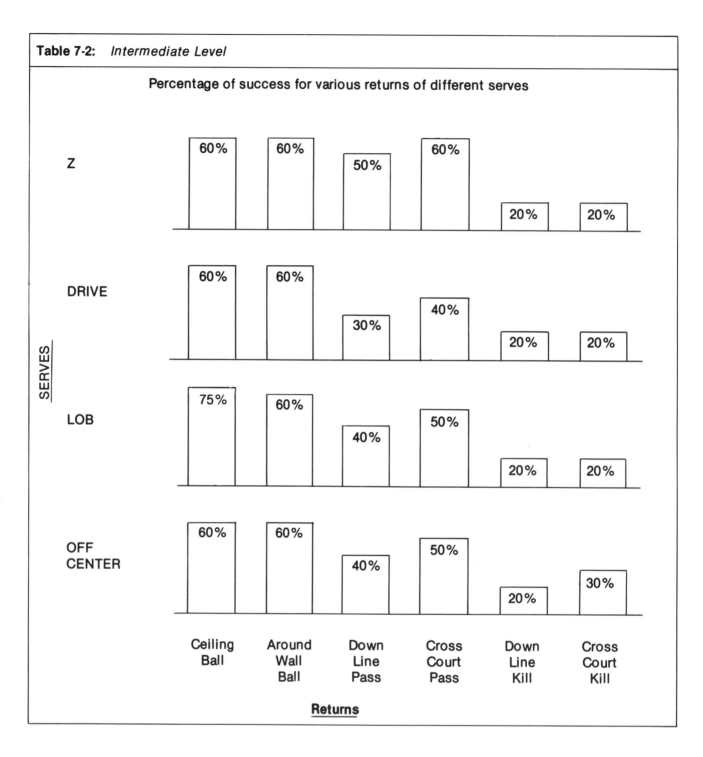

Percentage of success for various returns of different serves

SERVES

	Ceiling Ball	Around Wall Ball	Down Line Pass	Cross Court Pass	Down Line Kill	Cross Court Kill
Z	60%	60%	50%	60%	20%	20%
DRIVE	60%	60%	30%	40%	20%	20%
LOB	75%	60%	40%	50%	20%	20%
OFF CENTER	60%	60%	40%	50%	20%	30%

Returns

pend on a kill shot on two-out-of-ten attempts. Not an acceptable level of success. The ceiling ball, on the other hand, is equally effective in gaining center court and works eight-out-of-ten times.

Observe the server's tendencies. The server may telegraph play intentions, so have a friend observe the match while you concentrate on the ball. If possible, watch the opponent in an earlier match. Where does the server move after the serve? Some players will give up the first five points while watching the opponent's tendencies. With this information, they will hit serve returns which exploit these tendencies later (see Diagrams 7-2 to 7-5).

Practice each serve return from the same serve. For example, on the Z-serve, cut the ball off before 34 ft. on the side wall. Return down-the-line or crosscourt according to which direction the server turns. A right-handed server hits the Z and turns with the serve. So cut the ball off before the side wall, and return the serve down-the-line (see Diagram 7-6). If the server turns to the left, away from the ball on the

Table 7-3: *Advanced Level*

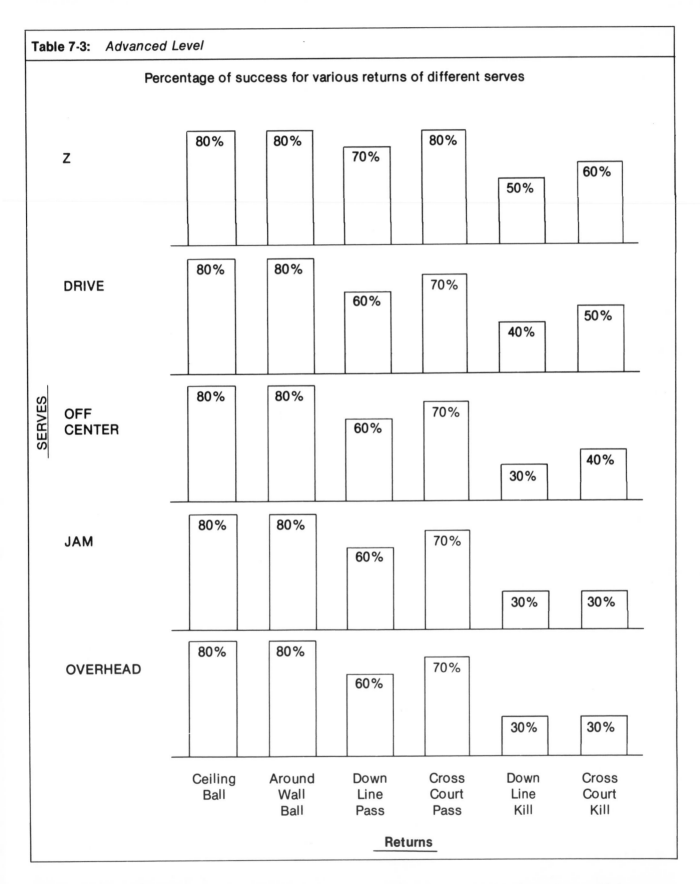

Percentage of success for various returns of different serves

SERVES

	Ceiling Ball	Around Wall Ball	Down Line Pass	Cross Court Pass	Down Line Kill	Cross Court Kill
Z	80%	80%	70%	80%	50%	60%
DRIVE	80%	80%	60%	70%	40%	50%
OFF CENTER	80%	80%	60%	70%	30%	40%
JAM	80%	80%	60%	70%	30%	30%
OVERHEAD	80%	80%	60%	70%	30%	30%

Returns

serve, cut the ball off before it reaches the side wall, and hit your return cross court (see Diagram 7-7). Hit a ceiling ball if you can't cut the ball off. If the serve is going to hit the back wall, follow it until it drops into a high percentage zone for you. Use this information about the server, and the specific serve to determine the best return of serve possible.

y = you set up to return serve
o = opponent's serve position
x = opponent's position after serve
----- = path of the serve
——— = path of the return

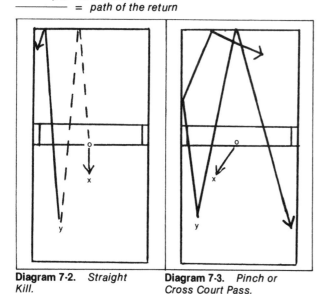

Diagram 7-2. *Straight Kill.*

Diagram 7-3. *Pinch or Cross Court Pass.*

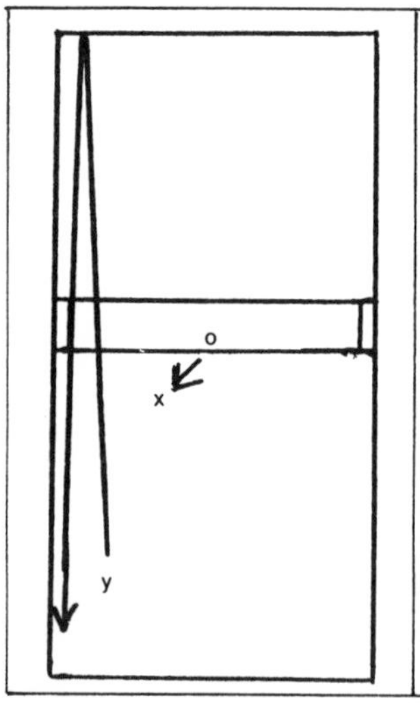

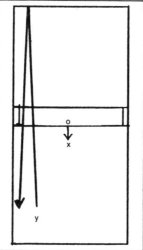

Diagram 7-4. *Ceiling Ball.*

Diagram 7-5. *Down-the-line Pass.*

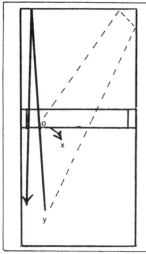
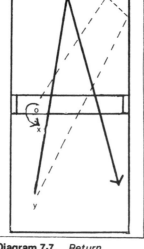

Diagram 7-6. *Return of Z-Serve Down the Line.*

Diagram 7-7. *Return of Z-Serve Crosscourt.*

TEACHING PROFESSIONALS: GUARD AGAINST COMMON ERRORS

Because the return of serve is the most difficult phase of racquetball to learn, your frustration level will be seriously tested. When frustration builds, your confidence suffers and poor execution follows. Other factors which contribute to poor serve returns are indecision, poor shot selection, and attempting shots you haven't practiced. The teaching pro should emphasize these basics. You should stay with what you know best, and don't change your mind in midserve. Don't look back! Concentrate on the coming serve, and execute a good return this time. The teaching pro should use Tables 7-1, 7-2, and 7-3 to educate club players about tournament level play.

WHAT TO DO WITH EACH SERVE?

The following are suggestions for practice returns based upon different types of serves, and solutions to problems students may encounter.

DRIVE SERVE

The drive serve is the most popular serve in racquetball. It is a power serve which can be accurately controlled by the server. It is senseless to think you can return most drive serves offensively. Many of professional racquetball players return the drive serve to the ceiling unless the ball is poorly served. As the charts indicate, the ceiling ball has an unusually high percentage return for all levels of play.

Look through the ball to the front wall if you are having difficulty picking up the drive serve when the server is in the middle of the service box. If you see the ball hit the front wall, the ball is coming to the right side. If you cannot see the ball hit the front wall, the ball is going to the left side. A good server can disguise the serve so you may not have time to react if you are watching the ball.

A little-known but effective technique employed by several highly ranked pros is overplaying the forehand side of the court. This does not mean playing out of position, but rather, watching for the serve to come to the forehand side, then shooting a straight or crosscourt kill. The server will become wary of serving to your forehand. Predictably, the rest of the serves will come to the backhand. The receiver now plays the backhand side by going the the ceiling, unless the serve is poorly hit or comes off the back wall.

For example, the receiver is right-handed. The server hits a drive serve which caroms off the side wall toward the middle. The receiver should either switch from backhand to forehand grip and shoot it to the left front corner, or keep the backhand grip and hit the ball cross corner. Drive serves off the back wall should be shot straight into the front wall. As you gain confidence, you can anticipate the backhand serve, move as the ball is served, and shoot more offensive shots.

Many pros position for the drive serve, and play to hit the crack between the side and back walls. They are then ready with a short, quick backhand stroke which keeps the ball in play if the serve hits the crack. If the ball hits two walls, they turn around with their forehand for the easy kill.

LOB SERVE

The lob serve is the next most widely used serve in racquetball; it is best used against the blaster or the player who shoots everything. This serve is slow-paced and does not generate low returns. The only effective, aggressive return of a lob is to short hop or hit the ball out of midair for a down-the-line passing/kill shot. This is a difficult return to execute. Cutting off a lob on the fly or short-hop will force the server back faster without time to setup, allowing the receiver time to move into center court. Choose a spot behind the hash mark to attempt the cut off, either a short hop or fly. Turn sideways, use a short stroke, and put the ball down-the-line.

Some players advocate the crosscourt pass in this situation because of its easier execution. The crosscourt pass is directed to your opponent's forehand and it is easier for the server to cover. Do not hesitate while you are moving in. Hit a firm shot, then glide into center court. Do not worry about a hinder! The server must give ample room for your return.

The better percentage return for most players is the well-hit ceiling ball. Do not fool yourself into thinking you can kill a well-hit lob serve from 38 ft., especially with the server in front of the service line waiting for an easy rekill. When the lob serve does carry off the back wall, make your opponent pay the price by allowing the ball to drop into a lower contact zone and hitting an aggressive offensive shot.

Z-SERVE

The Z-serve will require greater judgment than either the drive or lob serves due to its speed, various angles, and heights the ball will take into the back court. The return of the Z-serve described earlier is an advanced technique used by top players.

Find the point on the side wall 34 ft. back from the front wall. If the ball hits the side wall in front of this point, you can effectively hit a straight pass/kill or pinch shot depending upon your contact height. If the ball is going to angle and hit the side wall deeper than 34 ft., cut it off with a ceiling ball. Do not permit the ball to hit the side wall that deep; otherwise, you will play yourself into a corner. If you should let the ball pass, be absolutely sure the ball will rebound off the back wall for a down-the-line pass/kill or crosscourt pass/kill.

JAM SERVE

The jam serve is primarily used as a doubles serve. However, it is finding a place in singles as a serve that will make you run for the ball. It can be used by the server to determine whether you are alert and can handle serves into your body. If you are as quick afoot as superman, let the serve go to the back wall and shoot a down-the-line kill. If you are a mere mortal, go to the ceiling.

DO NOT LET THE BALL HIT THE BACK WALL! This will force you to move in two different directions. Also, avoid reaching in front of your body to play the ball to the ceiling. You can only play the ball poorly. Let the ball come to you, turn sideways, and then play it to the ceiling. An offensive return for the jam serve is to play it out of midair down-the-line. The serve will come to you in the middle, and the server must move or be tattooed.

Z-LOB SERVE

The Z-lob serve is difficult to return offensively. Your opponent will have a sure point 90% of the time if you misjudge the ball. The Z-lob serve is difficult to gauge because the server can easily vary the height, speed, and direction on every serve.

The best strategy against this serve is a ceiling or around-the-wall ball. If you can cut this serve off before it hits the side wall, hit an around-the-wall ball. Otherwise, go to the ceiling. Do not let this serve hit the back wall for a setup unless the ball hits above 4 ft. The spin and sharp dropping angle of the ball will require more time and distance for you to execute an effective kill.

OFF-CENTER SERVES

Occasionally, you will play an opponent who stands to the extreme left or right of the service box. While this creates a lot of angles for you to handle, the server has given you center court position. This advantage can be exploited. The technique used by the pros is to watch the front wall, because many players will use front wall targets to direct their serves. This method is especially good when the server is at either side of the service box. The body position and motion will not telegraph whether the server will hit a drive serve down-the-line, drive crosscourt, or a Z-serve. Instead, watch the front wall, pick up the serve when it strikes the wall target, then react accordingly. Attempt a return which will make the server run the farthest from center court. This technique will quickly exhaust your opponent, and give you many easy shots.

A SIMPLE STRATEGY FOR THE ALL-AROUND GAME

If you anticipate a specific serve, select a suitable return and practice it mentally. Review your return options should the serve be a complete surprise. When you are in doubt or caught off-balance, remember to hit a ceiling ball. These mental pictures are known as the **RETURN OF SERVE ANTICIPATION THEORY** and should be used before every serve.

There are three situations which can occur on the serve return. When you correctly predict the serve, you should select a serve return, practice it mentally, then execute your shot! For example, if you can see that the server is about to hit a lob serve, you should mentally practice moving forward and short-hopping the ball down-the-line.

Be aware of a second situation; uncertainty of what the serve will be. **PLAN A SPECIFIC SERVE RETURN!** Review your options if the serve is a complete surprise. If the server is positioned on the left side of the service box, anticipate a Z-serve to the backhand. You should mentally practice cutting it off and going crosscourt with the return. Be prepared for a drive serve to the right and be ready to hit a return down the right side wall.

The third situation possible is when you have no idea about which serve to expect. Review your basic serve return strategy; kill or pinch to the right, ceiling ball to the left, etc. As the ball is served, choose an option, **STICK WITH IT,** and then execute it to the best of your ability.

SUMMARY

Each return of serve, when used at the proper time, should have a purpose. Do not skip the ball or give the opponent an easy rekill opportunity. Remember, the purpose of a service return is to regain center court position, force a rally, and exploit the server's tendencies. Take away their forehand serve if possible, and play backhand serves to the ceiling. Shoot only bad serves, not marginal ones.

Study the charts, and remember the high percentages! You should experiment and learn the range of your hitting zones. The beginner may find balls in the knee range difficult to kill. The advanced players may find they can hit a chin-high ball consistently for a good pass shot. Different players have different hitting zones. Learn yours and remember, do not beat yourself.

Face the Sidewall for Your Backwall Shot.

CHAPTER 8

BACK WALL PLAY

The game of racquetball can be simplified into four basic areas: the serve, return of service, back court play, and midcourt play. These areas strategically control 95% of the game. In addition, back wall shots can occur during the return of serve, back court play, and midcourt play. The importance of good back wall play cannot be stressed too strongly, because the primary objective in racquetball is to score points. An aggressive back wall strategy will win games.

Specifically, back wall shots should be limited to balls which cannot be played with a reasonable chance for offensive success from midcourt. As a rule of thumb, when in midcourt, any shoulder-high ball should be allowed to come off the back wall for an easier shot.

FOREHAND AND BACKHAND STROKE TECHNIQUE

The following fundamentals apply to both the forehand and backhand strokes. The proper technique for the forehand stroke (for a right-hander) starts with facing the right side wall. As the ball passes, the player moves from front to back. The distance a player moves to or from the back wall depends upon the bounce of the ball.

Compare the ball to an ocean wave. It begins to crest after it bounces off the floor and strikes the back wall. If a second bounce occurs, the wave has passed. The object is to place yourself just short of that crest or second bounce. This position will allow an advanced player to step into the ball with the swing, and play the ball consistently at calf or ankle height, resulting in added power. This low point of contact allows the player to shoot the ball on a level trajectory, which minimizes skipped balls, and usually leads to a kill or pass shot.

Beginners are advised to work on placing themselves consistently parallel to the arc of the ball and playing it in the lower thigh-to-waist hitting area. Intermediate players should establish a slightly lower ball contact zone. A good height to work with is lower thigh to upper calf area. The player should strive to hit the front wall at about the same height as the swing contact point. This level swing promotes development into an advanced player, or at least a far better player.

To prepare for the forehand swing, rotate your shoulder and step into the ball. Then snap your wrist, as you drive through the ball. Always keep the racquet in a ready position at the highest point of your backswing. As the ball passes the front foot, the timing is coordinated so you step into the target area. This kind of contact results in a solid hit off the front foot.

Backhand skills in racquetball are basically the same. It is imperative to maintain a ready position and proper location to strike the ball offensively. In the correct ready position, face the left wall and turn at the waist so your shoulders face the back wall. The racquet is drawn back to the highest point of the backswing. As the ball reaches the front foot, snap the wrist and follow through with your swing. Remember to place yourself close to the back wall, and parallel to the arc pattern of the ball so that when the ball rebounds off the back wall, it will come directly into the front foot contact zone.

Essentials of good back wall play include: correct body movement and alignment to the back wall, the proper setup at the back wall, and a low and compact swing, with a good wrist snap, plus forward body movement. Remember to maintain eye contact with the ball through the contact zone. Short steps and quick side steps will keep you on your toes. Move forward after the shot (see Pictures 8-1 to 8-5).

The correct body movement and alignment to the back wall bring you more retrieved balls. Face the back wall as you run. Do not run with your racquet arm extended. Be prepared to play the ball from either a running or stationary position. If time permits, position your feet, and cock your wrist. Hold your racquet shoulder-high, with your elbow close to your body in a low crouch position. **FACE THE SIDE WALL** which corresponds with the forehand or backhand shot (see Picture 8-1).

Setup distance from the back wall is a judgment which depends upon the speed, height, and angle of the ball. Do not follow the ball to the back wall. Instead, select an area where you believe the ball will come out to your contact zone. Stay on your toes, and make your final body adjustments just before you hit the ball.

The drills which follow, if practiced correctly, will help develop correct body movement, stroke mechanics, and judgment for successful back wall play.

Photo 8-3. *Low Compact Swing.*

Photo 8-1. *Face Sidewall.*

Photo 8-4. *Eye Contact with Ball Through Contact Zone.*

BEGINNERS: DEVELOP TIMING, RHYTHM, AND JUDGMENT

THE BACK WALL TOSS is a drill which develops rhythm to move the body through a shot. For your forehand shot, set up 6" from the back wall and face the right side wall if you are right-handed. Hold the ball in your left hand and toss it **STRAIGHT** at the back wall about 3 ft. high. The ball should rebound **STRAIGHT** out and pass approximately 6" to 9" in front of your body.

Photo 8-2. *Take Short Steps.*

Photo 8-5. *Move Forward After the Shot.*

Shuffle sideways on your toes in synchronized rhythm to the movement of the ball. Permit the ball to bounce once, then let it drop a second time, and catch it with your left hand, with the catch occurring about ankle-high, slightly inside your left foot. This should correspond to the contact point if you had hit the ball. Your body should follow through the contact point at least one full step. Finish facing the front wall with your follow-through and move forward into center court position. You should now be 8 ft. to 10 ft. from the back wall. Repeat this drill until the motion of your body and the ball are one.

The next phase is to repeat the above procedure. Bring your racquet back, rotate the shoulders forward, and swing the racquet as if to hit the ball. Allow the racquet to meet the ball in your left hand at the contact point. Remember to keep moving one full step through the contact point in the direction of the shot.

The last phase of the drill is to shoot the ball straight to the front wall. Remember to remove your left arm from the path of the swinging racquet and follow-through. The front wall target should be straight ahead and 1 ft. high. All variations and sequences of this drill should be repeated with the backhand. **THE**

MAJOR POINT OF THE DRILL IS TO KEEP THE CONTACT POINT FURTHER IN FRONT OF THE BODY TOWARD THE FRONT WALL.

Good timing involves your changing directions, and now running forward to hit the ball. A variation of the back wall toss drill involves standing at the short line facing the back wall. Throw the ball at the back wall approximately 8 ft. high. Begin running toward the back wall, then change direction and move forward, catching the ball at the contact point with your left hand as you turn your body.

Repeat the drill until you can change directions easily and your body movement coincides with the ball. Vary this drill by moving closer to the back wall and throwing the ball lower off the back wall. The next step is to hit the ball straight to the front wall. Remember to follow through with a forward stroke after the shot, and face the front wall.

Judgment in the correct selection of the spot where the ball, the body, and the racquet head meet to form the contact point for any shot is fundamental. Stand at the short line facing the front wall and hit the ball into the front wall hard enough to make it rebound off the back wall in the air. Then run to the area where you think the ball will land after it has hit the back wall and bounced once. Set your body to play the ball correctly. First, however, catch the ball in your hand as before. Finding the correct spot, and setting up for the swing are more important than the actual shot. Once you learn to anticipate the correct spot, start hitting the ball to the front wall.

INTERMEDIATE PLAYERS: DEVELOP A STROKE WHICH GENERATES POWER FROM THE WRIST

Intermediate players should have sufficient form and consistency to practice **GAME SITUATION DRILLS.** These drills will develop a good back wall shot. The first drill is to repeat the back wall toss series with the added difficulty of hitting the ball before it bounces. Repeat the toss and catch, the toss, swing and catch, and the toss and hit since the drill timing is changed. Do not allow the ball to hit the floor.

The above situation will occur frequently during a game when the ball has bounced once before reaching the back wall. Your mastery of this drill will enable you to develop a low-short stroke. The front wall target should be straight ahead, 3" to 9" high.

Another excellent game situation drill for you is to hit ceiling balls off the back wall. The forehand can be mastered with little difficulty. Practice letting the ball drop to 3" to 6" before hitting it. Then hit the front wall 3" to 6" high. Hitting ceiling balls off the back wall with your backhand is a more difficult kill. Stay close to the back wall in a tight crouch with your racquet back and your wrist cocked. **REMEMBER — KEEP YOUR EYES ON THE BALL!**

The movement of your eyes, the swing of the racquet, and the direction of the ball should form a single line off the back wall. Begin your swing as soon as the ball strikes the back wall, then snap your wrist through the ball as you follow through. The contact point for a good backhand shot is ankle-high and slightly outside your right foot. Your body should continue to move through the contact point.

The wrist drop drill is important to the game of racquetball. Most racquetball players overlook the drill since its execution is difficult. The benefits from mastery of this drill are enormous. Improved back wall play, retrieval ability, and midcourt success will follow. A complete description of the Wrist Drop Drill can be found in Chapter Six.

ADVANCED PLAYERS: USE SHOT SELECTION TO DEFEAT THE OPPONENT'S COURT POSITION

Shot variety and flexibility are key skills for the advanced player. The advanced player has mastered a variety of shots off the back wall. The advanced player, too, is flexible enough to exploit an opponent's court position with the correct shot. Now practice your back wall shots without a bounce.

Having mastered the straight kill, the advanced player is ready to expand the shot repertoire. First, practice a back wall shot which is angled toward the front wall so the return is directed towards the closest back wall corner. Practice at a distance of 4 ft. to 10 ft. from a corner toward the middle of the back wall. The angle shot or passing/kill shot is tossed off the back wall similar to the straight kill. The ball should hit the front wall 3" to 9" high and angle to the corner between your forehand and the side wall.

To judge the correct angle, select a point on the back wall halfway between your racquet head and the (forehand) back wall corner. Envision the same point on the front wall and let your body movement flow in the direction of

that point through the shot. **DO NOT TRY TO ANGLE THE BALL WITH YOUR ARM SWING.**

The next shot is the pinch shot. From different points on the back wall (1 ft. to 10 ft.), toss the ball as before, and hit the ball off the side wall. If hit correctly, the ball will carom off the front wall and bounce twice before reaching the opposite side wall. The point on the side wall where the ball should strike varies with the point on the back wall where the shot originated. As a rule of thumb, the closer you are to the side wall, the further back the ball should strike on the side wall. Remember, your body motion is toward the point on the side wall where the ball should hit.

The crosscourt passing/kill shot is the next shot to master. This shot is similar to the passing/kill shot above. The ball, however, is directed crosscourt and finishes in the opposite back wall corner. Remember, use your body motion to direct the path of the ball. "Do not overcompensate the direction of the shot with your arm swing."

The next shot in this series is the splat shot. This shot requires great power, and the correct form for its execution. This shot is used when the ball is 1 ft. or closer to the side wall. Shoot the ball as hard as possible into the side wall while slicing the face of the ball. The spin generated by this slice should shoot the ball to the front wall with unpredictable spin. The ball will remain in front court and die close to the front wall if you executed it properly.

The last shot is the corner turnaround shot. This shot will permit retrieval when the ball hits the crack in the back wall corner and caroms, shooting out behind you unexpectedly, or jams you for a winner. Right-handed players in the return of serve position should position themselves approximately 3 ft. from the back wall and 6 ft. from the left side wall. Use the backhand grip with the racquet back and crouch low to play the ball (see Picture 8-6).

You are now in position to play the ball if it should hit the crack and shoot out (see Picture 8-7). If the ball hits the side wall, back wall, and carries toward midcourt, turn with the ball and play it with your forehand (see Pictures 8-8 and 8-9). Your shot can be angled to any point on the front wall. This shot is extremely difficult for your opponent to cover.

To practice this shot from the rally, position yourself in midcourt at 25 ft. Face the back wall, tap the ball into the right side wall, and run toward the backhand corner. Prepare yourself to play either the shot which rebounds straight off the back wall, or hits the side wall for a corner turnaround shot.

Photo 8-6.   *Use Backhand Grip With Racquet Back.*

Photo 8-8.   *Turn With Ball and Use Forehand.*

Photo 8-7.   *Ball Hits Crack & Shoots Out.*

Photo 8-9.   *Follow Through to Front Wall Target.*

Once you have mastered the straight kill, passing/kill shot, pinch shot, crosscourt passing/kill shot, splat shot, and corner turn-around shot with the forehand, repeat the drills with your backhand. These drills are stationary.

DYNAMIC MOVEMENT DRILLS THOUGH ARE ALSO ESSENTIAL FOR GAME SITUATION PRACTICE. The following are two game situation drills designed to improve back wall skills.

KILL AND CLOSE DRILL

Put yourself in the return of serve position. Toss the ball off the back wall, then hit the ball to the front wall from a stationary position, and run toward the front wall. The ball should rebound to center court. Now hit a second front wall shot to represent the server playing your return of serve. Continue running to the front wall playing the ball a third time. "The ball may bounce more than once." Shoot your third shot into either corner. The most common mistake is to stop running. You must continue to run through this entire three-shot series. The third shot is a rekill of the server's kill attempt (see Diagram 8-1).

Do not underestimate the importance of this drill. Repeated practice will teach you to play the ball on the run. This drill is also a great physical conditioner. You will win more matches if you learn to combat the opponent's kill attempt.

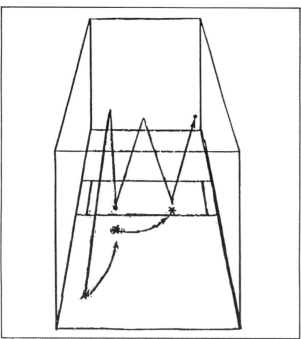

Diagram 8-1. *Kill and Close Drill.*

CONTINUOUS BACK WALL VOLLEY DRILL

The continuous back wall volley drill is simply shooting the ball repeatedly from the back wall out of midair. Begin by tossing the ball off the back wall and hitting a straight kill shot to the front wall. Immediately anticipate a position on the back wall where the ball will rebound. Allow the ball as many bounces as needed to bounce off the back wall again, and then hit another kill off the wall in the air.

Repeatedly play the ball off the back wall. Remember that skipped balls and double bounces do not stop play. Keep yourself moving and setting up at the back wall. You will get a great workout and develop a better feel for back wall play. In addition, you will also develop a winning stroke that is quick, low, and efficient.

SHOT SELECTION STRATEGY

The last section focuses on shot selection in relation to your opponent's position. Divide your opponent's position into three possible areas; front, mid and back court (see Diagram 8-2). Use crosscourt or passing/kill shots if the opponent is in front court since the opponent is covering pinch, splat, and kill shots. If the opponent is in midcourt, use the pinch or splat shots; the opponent is covering passing/kill shots. If the opponent is in back court, use the straight kill shot, the easiest shot to execute.

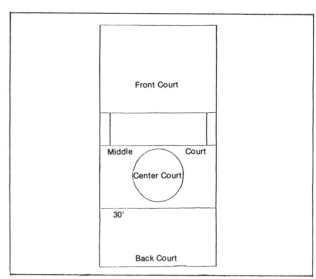

Diagram 8-2. *Areas of the Court.*

TEACHING PROFESSIONALS: EMPHASIZE GOOD FUNDAMENTALS

Teaching professionals should emphasize the fundamentals of good back wall play. Fundamentals include correct body movement and line to the back wall, proper setup at the back wall, a low and compact swing, a strong wrist snap, forward body movement in the direction the ball should travel, and eye contact through the contact zone.

Errors in judgment and technique are common in both the backhand and forehand, making the back wall one of the highest anxiety-inducing zones in racquetball. Here are some common problems:

1. Misjudment of the arc of the ball. This mistake is a common one. The player stands too close to the back wall and chases the ball down. The player frequently hits off balance, forcing shots to be played too high. The ball falls short of the ideal spot to hit a downswing.
2. Standing beyond the arc of the ball. A misjudgment of the rebound occurs, which forces you to reach backwards for each shot while shifting your weight backwards. The only means of recovery is for you to hit the ball into the back wall while unbalanced.
3. Racquet unprepared. This forces the player to take a quick incomplete swing which results in a variety of returns. Have your students practice swinging in the mirror and observe where the swing starts downward. This is the point of preparation.
4. The ball not dropping low enough into your contact zone. The result is a high shot which is easily covered by the opponent.
5. The ball too close to your body. Your arm swing will jam your body movement and affect your balance.
6. Starting too far from the ball. Your arm will straighten which greatly reduces power and control of the shot.

Consistent shots are the result of a powerful grooved swing, which means good position from the back wall, early racquet preparation, and patience in letting the ball drop to approximately the same height every time.

Position yourself with care. Consider the liveliness of the ball and the speed of the court surfaces. Slow balls and dead walls will greatly reduce the number of back wall shots. Any back wall shot will drop quickly. Fast balls and court surfaces, however, cause the ball to bounce higher and farther from the back wall. Adjust your body position accordingly, and remember to stay on your toes.

Anticipate the opponents next shot.

CHAPTER 9

ANTICIPATION — KEY TO WINNING

Good anticipation is the mental skill that will improve your racquetball ability, and enable you to defeat stronger opponents. Racquetball is just like any fast-moving game, and your ability to anticipate your opponent's shots can gain you the extra split second which allows you to reach more balls, neutralize your opponent's strategy, and setup quicker for your shots. Any discussion of anticipation must include a thorough description of the importance of center court position, an integral part of racquetball (see Chapter Six).

CENTER COURT STRATEGY

If you are a beginner, focus your movements around center court. In time, the game will come to you. Nearly every one of your movements will be confined to a coverage area that encompasses 2 to 12 ft. behind the service line and to within 3 ft. of the side walls (see Diagram 9-1). Speed, size, and stretching ability will determine how effectively you can cover this area. Correct center court play will enable you to be in a better position to retrieve shots in the rear 10 ft. of the court, and to cut off passing shots within 3 ft. of the side walls.

Anticipate the next shot as soon as you complete the follow-through of your serve! Move into center court in relation to where the ball is travelling and according to the location of your opponent (see Diagram 9-2). A rule of thumb is to position yourself on the side of the court where you hit the ball.

Move into center court position as quickly as possible, and setup to hit the ball with good body form while watching both the ball and your opponent. "Do not run a circle pattern!" You must follow the ball into the proper position after you serve. Do not overplay the center court position when you are covering normal shots because a strong opponent will win most rallies and make you look foolish. Generally, your court position should cover the pass shot. Remember, the most basic rule on all court coverage is **KEEP YOUR EYE ON THE**

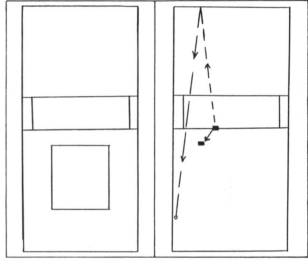

Diagram 9-1. *Center Court Quadrant.*

Diagram 9-2. *Relocate to Center Court Area.*

BALL AT ALL TIMES! Your eyes will start all of your movement on the court, and most of your misses originate when you take your eyes off the ball.

WATCH YOUR OPPONENT

Watching the ball is essential for you to make good contact with the ball. Expand your field of vision to include your opponent when it is his/her turn to hit the ball. Watch your opponent begin to setup on the shot. If your opponent is hitting from the left side of the court, turn slightly to your left so you can watch over your shoulder as the ball comes into the opponent's racquet. At the same time, study the opponent's body position and swing. You must now know whether to anticipate either a defensive shot like the ceiling ball, or an offensive shot like the kill or pass. You have a split second to decide. Most beginners make no attempt to disguise their intentions; the advanced player hits several different shots from the same swing.

You might not be able to determine exactly where your opponent is going to hit the ball, but you can anticipate when the ball is going to be hit and the probable center court action required by you. Be prepared to retrieve the shot, place it where it will do the most good, and put the ball away when you can. As the match progresses, you should improve your ability to anticipate what your opponent will do. The same shot patterns will occur more frequently, which will allow you to anticipate, and capitalize on, your knowledge of your opponent's game by positioning yourself where the ball will land.

SHOT SELECTION BY SITUATION

Many play situations repeat during a racquetball game. Be aware of these patterns so you can select the correct shot to win the rally. For example, if your opponent has a tendency to kill the return of serve, use a lob serve and cover the kill. If the opponent attempts to cut off the lob serve, take a deeper drop into center court, and protect against the pass shot. If the return is to the ceiling, hurry to the back wall, and take a quick look (using your peripheral vision) to see if the opponent is covering deep or short, left or right. Select the percentage shot which will counter your opponent's position! Table 9-1 is a guide for beginners to select the percentage shot. Memorize this chart, master the shots, and implement the strategy during games.

ANTICIPATION OFF THE SERVE

Intermediate players must realize that a good mental game means not telegraphing your intentions to your opponent. Learn to serve from the middle of the court, with your body position slightly to one side so you contact the ball at midcourt. Practice serving to both sides

of the court, and develop at least two service motions, control and power when contacting the ball for all basic serves (see Chapter One).

After you serve the ball, step back two or three steps out of the service box toward where the serve was directed. The angle of your body position should align with the opposite front corner and your opponent's approximate point of contact with the ball. The only way to determine the point of contact is to watch the receiver and the ball. This move will help you anticipate your opponent's shot, give you good position, and protect your back from a hinder (see Diagrams 9-3 & 9-4).

Charlie Brumfield believes you should analyze your opponent's swing on the return of serve. Where does opponent contact the ball? Does the opponent take a full backswing and follow through? Is the swing flat-horizontal or pendulum-vertical? Devise your serving strategy to take advantage of his/her tendencies. A

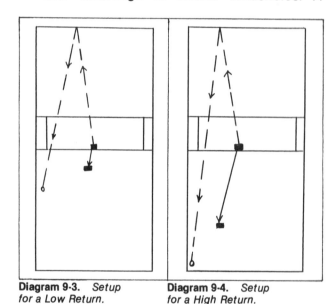

Diagram 9-3. *Setup for a Low Return.*   Diagram 9-4. *Setup for a High Return.*

Table 9-1:	*Beginners Guide for Shot Selection*			
		YOUR OPPONENT'S POSITION		
		FRONT COURT	**MIDDLE COURT**	**BACK COURT**
YOUR POSITION ABOUT TO HIT THE BALL	**FRONT COURT**	Down-The-Line	Diamond Pass	Straight Kill
	MIDDLE COURT	Down-The-Line	Straight Kill	Straight Kill
	BACK COURT	Ceiling Ball	Ceiling Ball	Ceiling Ball Straight Kill

horizontal swing will mean more control into the corners from Z-serves and angled shots. A vertical swing will mean more power down the lines with drive serves. Watch how opponent sets up to hit the ball, then shift your eyes to the front wall where you believe the shot will hit. Imagine before your opponent ever hits the ball where the return is likely to come from. You should be moving in that direction already, flowing toward the spot where you will make final contact with the ball; it is easier to make adjustments while you are moving.

Anticipation of this kind is fine, but the advanced player will have to do a lot more. Strategy is as important as anticipation. Maintain a variety of serves so your opponent never really knows what to expect from you. When you become too predictable and fall into a pattern, you give your opponent the edge. Never serve the same serve twice in a row.

Key factors in your positioning after the serve include the type of shot you hit, where your opponent hits from, what type of shot the opponent is likely to hit, and their capabilities and tendencies with that shot. A top player can cover an area in center court which gives him/her a position for covering several low shots. For example, you serve a low drive serve to the left rear corner. You know that your opponent's tendency is to attempt a straight kill, so you should position yourself in the front left quadrant of center court to give yourself a play on the straight kill, down-the-line pass, pinch, and reverse pinch (see Diagram 9-5). As you watch the ball, try to anticipate the shot you have given your opponent. Watch opponent setup over the ball, and position yourself to cut off the cross-court angle. Then evaluate the scoring potential from that particular spot on

the court to make a final adjustment in your court position.

If your opponent is forced to hit a shot from midair while on the run in the rear left side of the court, you should position yourself in the left rear quadrant of center court. Your opponent has little chance of hitting a flat kill against you (see Diagram 9-6). **USE YOUR HEAD!** If your shot caroms off the right side and back walls prior to the actual shot, you should anticipate a good kill shot attempt from your opponent. You need to adjust your position to the front right quadrant of center court (see Diagram 9-7).

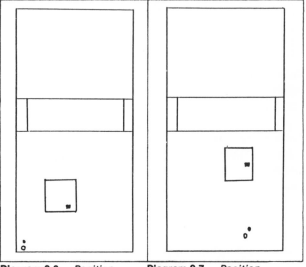

Diagram 9-6. *Position Yourself in Left Rear Quadrant.*

Diagram 9-7. *Position Yourself in Front Right Quadrant.*

SERVE RETURN BY ANTICIPATION

During the return of serve, if the ball can be played below your knees, hit it offensively (pass shot); if the ball must be taken above the knees, play it defensively (ceiling ball). A more definite method of shot selection based on anticipation is offered in Table 9-2. Your position on the return of serve will usually be in the back court. The exception is if you run to middle court and shoot the serve out of midair and/or short hop the ball. Anticipate opponent's position after his/her serve, and select a shot which counters this position (ceiling ball or pass shot). You can accomplish this by watching the server for a moment, by having a friend watch the server, or by remembering what happened earlier in the match.

Charlie Brumfield believes that you should gamble on the return of the serve when your opponent is winning. Choose a side, begin moving in that direction when your opponent is about to serve the ball, and shoot the return of serve. It is better to be aced several times if you

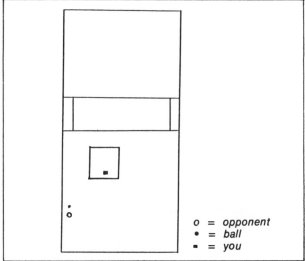

o = opponent
• = ball
■ = you

Diagram 9-5. *Position Yourself for Straight Kill.*

Table 9-2: *Shot Selection for the Return of Serve*

		YOUR OPPONENT'S POSITION		
		FRONT COURT	**MIDDLE COURT**	**BACK COURT**
YOUR POSITION ABOUT TO HIT THE BALL	MIDDLE COURT	Down-the-Line Diamond Pass	Straight Kill Pinch Shot V Pass Diamond Pass	None
	BACK COURT	Down-the-Line Ceiling Ball	Ceiling Ball V Pass	Ceiling Ball Pinch Shot Straight Kill

anticipate wrongly, than to be run into the ground because you can't gain the offensive on the serve.

Steve Keeley has said that the best offensive return of serve is to move up and cut the ball off on the fly. Your volley shot need not be a perfect pass or kill because the server will not have time to setup and so must retrieve the ball on the run. This is especially good when returning Z-serves and lob serves. You can anticipate the serve by watching the server's motion and body movement after the serve. Form a mental image of that position when you are returning their future serves. Don't forget to watch the ball!

ANTICIPATION DURING THE RALLY

According to Keeley, anticipation during a rally may be summed up in one simple statement: expect the ball to be hit away from you and directed to take you out of midcourt. Steve Strandemo thinks it is better to anticipate most of the returns to your backhand, then you must be mentally prepared for the shot you are going to return. First, lean to the backhand side, then switch to your backhand grip, and move your body into a proper hitting position.

Strandemo continues by saying that good anticipation begins with watching your opponent's swing, and opponent's body position as he/she hits the ball. An open stance usually means the contact point will be in front of their body, so the ball will go crosscourt. A close stance shifts the contact point to your back foot and directs the ball into the near side wall. The body position for a ceiling ball will be high, while a very low body position is needed for the kill shot.

Anticipation during the rally is as important as at any other time. Dave Peck advices you to trust your instincts as to where the next shot is going, and begin moving into position slightly before the opponent strikes the ball. Stay on your toes at all times, with knees bent slightly, and your feet shoulder-width apart. Keep your back straight and carry your racquet waist-high. If you switch grips, hold the grip which matches the side of the court the ball will be coming from. If you are in center court, most retrievable balls will come within one or two long steps and a stretch of your body. Practice this footwork pattern in different directions from center court, because efficient body movement will save you valuable time and energy, while increasing your ability to rekills the ball.

Brumfield states that you should use the momentum of the shot to carry yourself forward into a better court coverage position. You should cover the crosscourt shots, since 75% of all shots during a normal match go to a crosscourt coverage pattern either by a pinch or crosscourt pass. **REMEMBER, CROWDING IS ILLEGAL!** A better alternative is to flow in behind your opponent, tip-toeing and cutting in at the last second, one way or the other. This gives you more balance, a natural block after your shot, and a chance for a hinder. You are also less likely to be hit with a racquet or called for an avoidable hinder.

Covering the crucial surrounding court zones increases your chances of retrieving your opponent's shots more often. Center court position gives you plenty of swing and retrieval room for killing into the corners, killing balls on the fly, and hitting crosscourt or down-the-line pass shots, ceiling or Z-balls. If you are quick and anticipate the crosscourt pass correctly, it will be easy to step into the crosscourt lane, intercept the ball, and kill it in the closest corner.

If your opponent gets a setup on his/her forehand side and tries to pinch the right corner or go crosscourt, you should shade to left of center. If opponent hits a forehand down the line, straight kills, or uses a crosscourt pass cover down the line, this gives you more time to recover for the crosscourt shot. If an opponent hits everything crosscourt, play to the far left of center court and deep enough not to be passed. This situation occurs frequently with beginning and intermediate players and can easily be exploited. If your opponent repeatedly beats you with one shot, watch him/her in action against other players to observe how they neutralize this shot.

Randy Stafford asserts that the secret to winning every rally rests on your ability to determine your opponent's position and your execution of specific shots to defeat that position (see Table 9-3). A player can only be considered advanced when he has mastered all the shots shown below and uses them at the proper time during a match.

ANTICIPATION OFF THE BACK WALL

The following theory of anticipation outlines how to handle back-wall play. Low balls off the back wall will be killed by any good player. Balls that rebound high, above 3 ft., will tend to go crosscourt because, as the opponent lets the ball drop for a kill shot, the contact point with the ball moves in front of his/her body, thus directing the ball crosscourt. Covering these situations should by now be a matter of common sense to you.

BRUMFIELDS DEEP ZONE THEORY

Brumfield offers his deep zone theory for helping the advanced player to cover his/her opponent. The key to playing the deep zone is flowing forward as your opponent hits the ball. Starting from the deep position, you should already be moving up on the ball. Don't be so overanxious that you over-anticipate the ball and only get to poke at it. You can't move as gracefully or efficiently as someone coming from the back to move onto the ball and hit it hard every time. The **DEEP ZONE WITH ARRIVAL HIT TIME THEORY** is Charlie's name for this theory.

Table 9-3: *Shot Selection During the Rally*				
		YOUR OPPONENT'S POSITION		
		FRONT COURT	**MIDDLE COURT**	**BACK COURT**
YOUR POSITION ABOUT TO HIT THE BALL	FRONT COURT	V Pass Down-the-Line Diamond Pass	Pinch Shot Drop Shot Z Ball Diamond Pass	Pinch Shot Drop Shot Straight Kill Reverse Pinch
	MIDDLE COURT	V Pass Down-the-Line Diamond Pass	V Pass Straight Kill Pinch Shot Reverse Pinch Diamond Pass	Straight Kill Pinch Shot Reverse Pinch Fly Kill
	BACK COURT	V Pass Down-the-Line Ceiling Ball Around the Wall Ball	V Pass Ceiling Ball Pinch Shot	Straight Kill Ceiling Ball Pinch Shot Reverse Pinch Overhead Shot

Here are a couple of other pointers: first, position yourself during the rally to dictate where your opponent is going to hit the ball. That does not mean positioning yourself to block the opponent's shot. Stay close to the opponent showing one coverage. Then, at the moment of contact, move for your crosscourt coverage. Second, **BE PREPARED FOR THE SUNDAY SHOT.** Every player has a favorite shot that he/she is confident of hitting, especially under pressure. Know these shots, cover them, and react to put the ball away.

CHARTING YOUR OPPONENT'S WEAKNESSES

The semi-pro player can take the game one step further by studying the habits of other semi-pro players. An excellent system for studying a player's habits is presented in Chapter 15. This details how to scout and record your opponent's strengths and weaknesses. Also, it will show you how to analyze and prepare a game plan which will defeat your opponent.

SUMMARY

Two factors always present in racquetball should be the first things you think about before a match. First, every player has weaknesses relative to the rest of their game. The sooner you detect these weaknesses, the sooner you can anticipate and take advantage of them. Second, you must come to an understanding with yourself of your skill level. **WHAT ARE YOUR CAPABILITIES?** What can you do and what can you not do? Decide before the match how you are going to control the tempo. Are you going to play a fast running game, or a control ceiling game? Determine the areas on the court in which you feel most confident so you can concentrate on your game in those areas. learn to anticipate your opponent's returns, and force your returns toward the area on the court which suits your strengths.

The first few points of a match are for experimentation. Feel your opponent out. Try a variety of serves to see which serves cause them the most difficulty. Some serves will allow better returns than others, so discover them as soon as possible. Your serve should have two purposes. It should create difficulty for your opponent in returning the ball, and it should force the opponent into the type of return you desire. Then you may setup for the anticipated return.

As your opponent begins serving, watch him/her carefully. Vary your return of serve so that he/she cannot easily anticipate your return. Watch him drop into center court position after the serve to determine the best return to break serve. Does he/she handle every return equally well? Once you find his/her weakness, hit that shot, cover the best return, and wait for the bad return. Remember, if you keep your eyes on the ball, anticipate your opponent's shots, vary your returns, and play percentage shots, you will go a long way toward defeating an opponent.

Most rallies are won as a result of three occurrences: a skip ball, a kill shot, or a shot that takes advantage of poor court position. The first and second occurrences are the result of your opponent's racquet skill. The third relies solely upon your mental ability. Don't get caught out of position!

Do not run up front after every shot! This strategy may enable you to pick up a few kill shots, but your opponent will begin to hit a safer pass shot and defeat you every time. Do not play under your opponent's armpit. Opponent's follow-through will inhibit your body movement to the ball and, according to the rules, "there is no hinder on a follow-through." Do not lag in back court waiting to see your opponent put the ball away. You should also avoid running up your opponent's back, stamping your feet, or shouting during the rally. This behavior is illegal, and you are taking yourself out of the game mentally and physically. **CONCENTRATE!**

Concentrate on the Ball.

CHAPTER 10

CONCENTRATION ON THE BALL

"How can I increase my concentration on the ball for long periods of time?" This is a question that is often asked. The following story told by holy men in the East most effectively answers this question.

"A seeker after truth sought out a yoga master and begged him to help him achieve the enlightenment of perfect union with his true self. The Master told him to go into a room and meditate on God for as long as he could. After just two hours, the seeker emerged distraught, saying that he could not concentrate, since his mind kept thinking about his much beloved bull he had left at home. The Master then told him to return to the room and meditate on his bull. This time the would-be yogi entered the room and after two days had still not emerged. Finally the Master called for him to come out. From within, the seeker replied, (I cannot; my horns are too wide to fit through the door.) The seeker had reached such a state of concentration that he had lost all sense of separation from his object of concentration" (Gallwey, p. 92).

As silly as it may sound, one of the most practical ways to increase your concentration on the ball is to love it! Acquaint yourself with the racquetball; appreciate its qualities. Examine it closely and notice the fine line of the seam. Forget for a moment that you are holding a racquetball. Look anew at the shape, texture, and feel of the ball. Consider the inside of the ball and the importance of the hollowness. know the ball both intellectually and sensually. Your concentration will improve immeasurably.

Concentration is the act of focusing your attention! As your mind focuses on a single object, it becomes still. The relaxed mind concentrated upon the present will become calm. Concentration means keeping your mind in the here and now; this is the supreme art, and vital to all personal achievement. You cannot explore the limits of your ability in racquetball without learning how to concentrate; the game should be a marvelous medium through which to develop complete concentration skills.

All you need to practice your concentration skills is an appropriate object on which to focus attention. In racquetball, the most convenient and practical object is the ball. The most often repeated cue in racquetball is **WATCH THE BALL.** This instruction is an appeal to you to concentrate. Many players look at the ball or the general area surrounding the ball, but fall short of achieving true concentration. As they look at the ball, they are choosing a shot or contemplating a possible lost point. This is wasteful of energy. The concentrating mind does not let such distractions enter it; it is totally absorbed in the object of concentration.

CONCENTRATION DURING PRACTICE

Concentration on the court can be improved with practice. Watching the ball means focusing your attention only on the ball. The most effective way to deepen your concentration through sight is to focus on something subtle (a white line painted on the ball). The practice of watching the white line will produce some interesting results. After a short time, you will begin to see the ball much better. While looking at the white line, you will naturally watch the ball until it hits the racquet, and then begin to focus attention on the ball earlier. Watch the ball from the time it leaves your opponent's racquet until it meets yours.

Most players who practice seam-watching as a discipline find it helpful almost immediately. Their minds do often wander though! Anyone will have difficulty focusing on a single object for any extended period of time; however, the racquetball has one quality which makes it a good object for concentration, movement. Our minds are naturally attracted to objects in motion.

To concentrate is not to stare! Concentration is the fascination of the mind upon something outside itself. As shown in our parable, when love is present, the mind is drawn irresistibly toward the object of love.

Your concentration should be effortless and relaxed, not tense and purposeful. When you watch the white line of the ball allow yourself to fall into a state of relaxed concentration. If your eyes are squinting or straining, you are trying too hard. Let the ball attract your mind; then both your mind and muscles will remain relaxed.

Watching the ball's white line helps you to focus attention on the ball itself. Increased awareness of the flight of the ball as it moves toward and away from you is just as important. During a rally, focus on the particular trajectory of each shot. Notice the height of the ball as it hits the front wall, its speed, the angle at which it rises after bouncing, and the ball's angles off the side walls. Also observe whether the ball is rising, falling, or at an apex the instant before the racquet makes contact. Give the same careful attention to the trajectory of your own shot. Soon you will become aware of the rhythm of alternating shots during the rally. Your ability to anticipate will then increase. This rhythm, both seen and heard, holds the fascination for your mind, enabling it to focus for longer periods of time without distraction. Another hint: imagine yourself riding on the ball or becoming the ball's shadow. As long as the ball is in motion, so are you. If it moves right, so do you, if it goes left, so does its shadow. Low zone and you are low, high zone and you are floating on your feet to meet the ball.

RESTRICTION OF AWARENESS

You must also learn to focus your awareness in the present. The greatest lapses in concentration occur when we allow our minds to project to future events or dwell on past ones. How easily our mind absorbs itself in the world of "what ifs." What if I lose this point, we think, then I'll be behind 14-13. If I don't break serve, then I'll have lost the first game and probably the match. I wonder what Sue will say when she hears I lost to Adam. At this point a player frequently lapses into a fantasy about Sue's reaction to the news that he/she has lost to Adam. Meanwhile, in the present, the score is still 13-13, and you are barely aware that you are on the court. The conscious energy needed to perform at your peak in the present has been leaking into an imagined future.

Similarly, the mind often draws one's attention into the past. If the referee hadn't called that last serve short, the score would be tied, and I wouldn't be in this mess. The same thing happened to me last week, and it

cost me the match. I lost my concentration, then confidence, and now the same thing is happening again. I wonder why? In racquetball, before long you or your opponent will hit the ball, summoning you back to the present. However, part of your energy is left in the thought world of the past or future. The present is not seen with all of your awareness. Objects look hazy, the ball seems to come faster, appears smaller, and even the court seems to change. Keep your mind on the present, i.e., is the next shot coming to my forehand or backhand?

CONCENTRATION OFF THE COURT

To help you improve your focus on the present, Robert Ornstein describes a simple meditation technique to practice off the court. The general instructions for most beginning meditation exercises are similar; pay close and continuous attention to the meditation object (the ball). This exercise is more difficult than it sounds. Most beginners often lose awareness of the meditation object. Each time you notice that awareness has shifted from the object of meditation, return your attention to it. Regardless of the technique you employ, each session of meditation should last about half an hour. Meditation should be practiced twice a day, in the morning before the day's major work and again in the evening. Beginners should practice for less time and work up to about half an hour a day. As you progress, add more complicated exercises.

Those exercises which involve restriction of awareness, the focusing of attention on the object of meditation, or the repetition of a word, are called "concentrative meditation." All cultures have one similarity. Whatever the form or technique, the essence of meditation is an attempt to restrict awareness to a single, unchanging source of stimulation for a definite period of time. The successful achievement of this exercise is termed "one-pointedness of mind."

If the exercise involves vision, the meditator gazes at the object of meditation continuously. If the meditation is auditory, the sound or word is repeated over and over again, either aloud or silently. If the meditation consists of physical movement, the movement is repeated continuously.

Since the mind seems to have a will of its own, how can you learn to keep it in the present? By practice. There is no other way. Every time your mind starts to slip away, simply bring it back. Use a verbal cue, "ball."

Repeat the word "ball" continually while simultaneously fixing your eye on the ball. Off the court, practice another technique. First, make your mind blank, then close your eyes, and imagine the front wall of the court. Locate the ball on the front wall, and gradually move closer to the ball until you can seem the seam. Look past the seam to the texture and crevices on the ball's surface. This technique will significantly improve the length of your concentration on the ball.

The most effective means of increasing your concentration ability is through the practice of meditation. Timothy Gallwey relates a personal experience: "After practicing a certain technique of meditation for several months, I was surprised to find my alertness so increased that I could completely alter the style and tactic of my return of serve. Even against hard first years, I seemed to have the time needed to respond and pick up the ball just a split second after it bounced. There was no time for a backswing and no time to think about what I was doing. There would just be a calm concentration followed by a quick movement to meet the ball — initiated even before the ball had passed over the short line — a follow-through which gave direction and height to the ball, and then in the next instant I flowed into center court — well before the server" (Gallwey, p. 100).

You might think this tactic would be impossible against a really first-rate serve. Not true. This serve return can become a great advantage in tournament play after only several months of experimentation. The greater the use, the quicker and more accurate your reactions will become.

Concentration will seem to slow down time, giving you the necessary awareness to see and place the ball. Meeting the ball before it hits the side wall and cutting off the angle from a serve is a tremendous advantage. Reaching center court before the server controls this area is just as valuable. A minor revolution would occur in the game of racquetball if a top-flight amateur or professional were to perfect this technique. The longstanding advantage of the server would be reversed.

CONCENTRATION DURING A MATCH

Methods for your concentration development are best employed during practice, on or off the court. During a match, choose one object of concentration — whatever works best for you — and focus on it. For example, if the ball tends to keep you centered in the here and now, there is no need to focus on sound or movement. Merely playing a competitive match will frequently often help you concentrate. During a rally, you often find yourself in a state of deep concentration. You are only aware of what is happening at that instant.

The critical time is between points! After the last shot of a rally, the mind no longer focusing on the ball may wander. Thoughts of the score, your erratic backhand, business, the children, and dinner tend to siphon energy away from the present moment. It is getting harder for you to regain your previous level of concentration before the next point begins. Come back to the ball with your visual or verbal cue; "ball."

Remember, "the value of concentration becomes clear as we grow to understand that nothing can be enjoyed or appreciated if it cannot be known. Beauty cannot be enjoyed unless one can know it. Peace cannot be enjoyed unless it can be known. The same goes for love and truth — in fact, anything that is valued by people. By increasing the effective power of awareness, concentration allows us to shed more light on whatever we value, and to that extent enables us to know and enjoy it more" (Gallwey, p. 98).

Down Swing.

Snap Wrist Through Contact Zone.

Wrist Cocked.

Contact Ball at or Below Wrist Level.

CHAPTER 11

PRACTICE WITH YOUR MIND AND BODY

Mental practice is the systematic focusing of thought about your performance in some past or future athletic endeavor. Practice, while directed to future endeavors, relies on past performance. Many athletes use mental practice procedures to increase their learning speed and improve their performance. Mental practice means quietly and purposefully envisioning an imaginary motion picture of yourself. Unfortunately, very few players develop the ability to visualize events in such a clear and complete manner.

For example, while jogging, let your mind recreate a previous match. You should vividly recall each detail of every point as if you were reliving the game. A more practical use of this ability is to convert the past into the future. Imagine playing in the finals of the next tournament against a worthy opponent. Project yourself at 8-8 in the tie breaker, needing 3 points to win the championship.

Your serve; a drive serve to the left cracks out on the side wall to give you point 9. Next, you use a drive serve to the right, and your opponent returns a ceiling ball to your backhand. The ball was hit too hard, giving you a shot off the back wall. You setup at the back wall, and fire a backhand kill shot into the left corner for point 10. Then you serve a low hard Z-serve into the right corner. The ball sets up just enough to give your opponent an offensive opportunity. You gamble and charge the right front corner. He hits a pinch shot. You dive and rekill the ball for match point.

Mental practice is used extensively by coaches in gymnastics and diving. Practice procedures are often used to assist these athletes in their awareness of body position and movement through the recall of kinesthetic cues. These cues are then paired with visual images.

Athletes have reported remarkable improvement due to mental practice. For example, the Keeley Box Theory is the drill for corner kills. Steve Keeley created a drill that provides a better mental picture for kill shots to both the forehand and backhand corner. Imagine a 1 ft. × 1 ft. × 1 ft. box sitting in both front wall corners. As you attempt a corner kill, aim on any part of that imaginary box in the corner. This will give you a one foot margin of error. Any shot that hits somewhere in that area will be a winner.

Practice this drill by hitting ceiling ball setups and shooting forehands and backhands to both corners. Hit 20 balls to each side. You can place masking tape in the corner as a target. Improvements in your performance will lead to better concentration and confidence.

MENTAL IMAGERY VERSUS MENTAL PRACTICE

The mental practice of recalling sensations associated with improved performance is not new; you have probably already used visual imaging to facilitate an appropriate level of competitive tension. Some players psych themselves up in a competitive situation; others relax and imagine a peaceful, calm scene. Mental practice and simple imagery are not the same. By definition, practice involves the active study of an image or a series of images. In contrast, simple imagery means the ability to develop an image without analyzing its content. The difference is comparable to the difference between acting in a movie or merely watching it. Simply watching is not enough! Just looking at something does not involve conscious attempts at controlling your environment or tension levels.

MENTAL PRACTICE OFF THE COURT

Try the following test to practice your serve off the court. Sit at a table in a quiet room. You will need two pieces of 5-1/2-inch-by-11-inch paper, a pencil, and a blindfold. One piece of paper represents the floor of a racquetball court. Draw two horizontal lines to represent the serving box. On the left end of the serving box, tear the paper slightly. The tear will serve as a starting point when you are blinded. The second piece of paper is placed end to end with the first piece representing the front wall.

Put on the blindfold, and you are ready to begin. With pencil in hand, find the tear with your opposite hand. Imagine the shape of the court. Begin by writing the number 1 in the service box to represent where you will stand to serve a drive serve to the right. Next, move to the top of the paper, and write the number 1 to represent the front wall target for the same drive serve. Remember, this number will show both direction and height of the ball. Finally, move to the bottom of the paper and write a third number 1 to represent where the serve should finish. Repeat this drill for every serve, changing the number each time. Remove the blindfold when you have finished and connect the numbers. Determine whether your serves were hit correctly. This form of mental practice will give your serves greater accuracy and consistency on the court.

Kathy Williams suggests that you should sit quietly with your eyes closed before entering the court. Envision yourself playing a perfect game. Watch your kill shots roll out, your perfect pass shots, and your unreturnable serves. Erase all negative thoughts, and see yourself winning a big tournament. If you enter a tournament worrying about your shots and hoping to get lucky, you will lose the match. Find a quiet place before any important match, and practice your mental game.

MENTAL PRACTICE ON THE COURT

Use the mental technique of cueing the shot prior to its execution. For example, on a pinch shot, mentally tell yourself "pinch." The results are remarkable. In less dramatic situations, controlled studies indicate that mental rehearsal can be very effective, particularly for learning simple motor skills. Subjects were able to correct mistakes immediately and increase performance levels simply by visualizing a mistake.

The ability to use visual imagery as a memorization technique for large amounts of information has a special significance. Although speech could seem to be the obvious means of describing behavior, this process can be slow and laborious. Many plays in competitive sports occur at a tremendous rate of speed, limiting our ability to describe them in words.

For example, try describing the experience of a racquetball coming toward your head at 100 miles per hour! The limitations of verbal communication are now obvious.

LIMITING ATTENTION

The ability to use imaging and to recognize particular situations will sharpen your reflexes. Visualization will aid your memory. Visualize the whole, not just a group of impressions, and use the entire picture to remember the component parts. Any situation will contain a great deal of information that is irrelevant for your purposes. Train your mind to eliminate peripheral details and focus on what counts.

Many players make the same mistake repeatedly in similar situations. Through the visual recall of certain situations, you can train yourself to take mental pictures of your environment, allowing you to remember which shot an opponent used previously in a comparable situation. The rehearsal process analyzes the situation and selects the best spot for covering the shot.

There are cues in any situation that are critical determinants of successful performance. Being aware of these crucial cues will give you an advantage! As your basic skills are developed and become reflexive, these cues will no longer require your conscious attention. A beginning racquetball player must pay attention to the placement of the feet within the service box, the grip, and body position, while experienced players automatically assume a stance which feels right without checking specifics. They "know" their total feeling. This "knowing" feeling frees the mental process to focus on other factors. For example, an experienced racquetball player does not wait to see the ball in flight before reacting. He/she anticipates the opponent's movements and covers accordingly.

REHEARSAL PROBLEMS

Some players fail because they did not move back far enough into their behavioral chain of events. For example, your backhand shots are going crosscourt. You cannot seem to locate the cause of the problem. Is it your feet, your body position, or your follow-through? Instead of asking these individual questions, you should mentally begin at the beginning, reviewing each segment in your backhand stroke. Lo and behold, it was your backswing!

During practice, consider each physical element of each shot and how it feels. In a game though, your concentration and rhythm would be destroyed if you thought this much. Ideally, through reflection on your past performance and off-court rehearsal, you will learn what a good shot feels like. Conscious attention to all movements becomes unnecessary. **YOU JUST KNOW!**

Begin by actually practicing a court activity a few times. Pay attention to the feelings within the specific parts of your body at certain points during the activity. Practice each motion several times with a smooth, natural flow until completion. Don't be jerky, or self-conscious; you should flow through these exercises. You should now be able to sit down and recall each related feeling in your body as you performed the entire activity.

The steps that proceed from this awareness will help you determine your focal point. The trick is to become aware of both correct or incorrect performances, to learn to discriminate between the two. Mentally produce a composite picture of how your behavior looks and feels when you perform it correctly. Now comes the important step. The discrepancies you notice are your discriminative cues. Use these to correct your past errors as you mentally rehearse the best technique.

Maintain a receptive attitude during these rehearsals, relax! Observe your performance and feelings in an absorbent and objective manner. You are playing the role of both observer (coach) and participant (athlete). The coach calls attention to the important aspects of performance; the athlete listens, executes the movements, and then observes his/her feelings. To experience this procedure, assume the role of both the coach and athlete in your practice session

REHEARSE YOUR BACKHAND

Learn backhand techniques more easily by dividing them into segments. Give these segments descriptive terms, and then talk yourself through each step of the technique. You will improve your performance by imagining these segments in order, and by repeating the segment names in place of actual practice. Researchers have found that when you mentally rehearse a motor task, you fire the correct muscle groups in the correct order. Mental practice seems to help even if subjects are motionless.

Successful mental practice is a combination of both muscle relaxation and your skill in imagery. You must learn to relax your primary muscles; this is a prerequisite for skill imagery.

Muscle relaxation can be achieved by focusing your attention on the tensing and relaxing of each muscle. Tense a specific muscle for four seconds and relax for four seconds; use the biceps of the upper arm as an example, and follow these directions:

1. Bend right arm at the elbow. The hand should be near the shoulder.
2. Contract the biceps tighter and tighter.
3. Focus on tension in the right biceps.
4. Notice the feeling in the arm.
5. Relax by slowly lowering the hand.
6. Observe the absence of tension.
7. Notice the feeling of relaxation in the upper arm.
8. Repeat the movement once.
9. Follow the same directions for each muscle in the right arm and shoulder.

After your arm is relaxed, focus your attention on the backhand stroke. Close your eyes and concentrate on how to hit the shot. Relax and watch yourself stroke the ball. Slow the image down and rerun it one step at a time. Now break it into short, important segments which have been chosen with a racquetball coach. For example, break the backhand stroke into the following components:

1. Racquet grip
2. Backswing with elbow bent 90 degrees
3. Wrist cock
4. Body position to side wall
5. Shoulder rotation
6. Front foot forward at 45 degree angle to side wall
7. Front knee slightly bent
8. Weight shift
9. Arc of the forward arm swing
10. Wrist snap
11. Ball contact
12. Follow-through
13. Trailing leg

Determine the cues again for each segment which indicates a discrepancy between the successful and unsuccessful shot. Once these differences are identified, rehearse them several times to correct the discrepancy. For example, think several times of shifting your forehand grip to a backhand grip. Refrain from this rehearsal in competitive situations if you have already hit the ball correctly, and are working on consistency. Once the point is over, however, take time to rehearse the correction of your mistake. Use this rehearsal process only if you are able to practice it objectively. If you find yourself cursing while mentally making a correction, you may be increasing not reducing, your level of tension. This anger could easily be transferred into your next rally, interfering with your concentration and performance.

Your experience will appear in slow motion as fewer distractions intrude upon your mind. You are now immersed totally in the game and have lost all awareness of self. You flow with the activity and, only later, when normalcy returns, do you realize the extent of your involvement.

Through the use of mental rehearsal processes, you can train yourself to recognize the important cues in all competitive situations. By learning the important elements of racquetball and practicing your passive concentration, you will increase your awareness. The combination of mental awareness and practice will result in your greater involvement in each game. Finally, the awareness of the correct procedure in a competitive situation will help you to recognize your mistakes.

Learning to play racquetball well is more than mere physical activity. As in any sport, the relationship between mind and body is complex. Your skill may be either mental or physical, but if you have both skills, you will **WIN!**

The common assumption is that racquetball skills are the result of a lot of physical practice. Although physical practice is indispensable to attaining high skill levels, mental practice is also a means of increasing motor skill. Mental practice involves envisioning a definite performance within your imagination.

The effectiveness of mental practice is not surprising, given the normal process of learning racquetball. Thought is an integral part of such learning before, during, and after your physical practice on the court. This is especially true in gaining complex racquetball skills. Your goals and strategies must be determined in advance, with results evaluated, alternatives considered, and success or failure judged. Mental practice is an attempt to formalize each activity with your mind!

The advantage of mental practice is that you can mentally perform each racquetball skill perfectly 100% of the time. You will know beforehand the correct performance of each skill which will accelerate your learning process.

Through mental practice, you can increase your ability to concentrate, gain self-confidence, improve your performance, and increase your opportunity to realize a peak experience (ultimate pleasure).

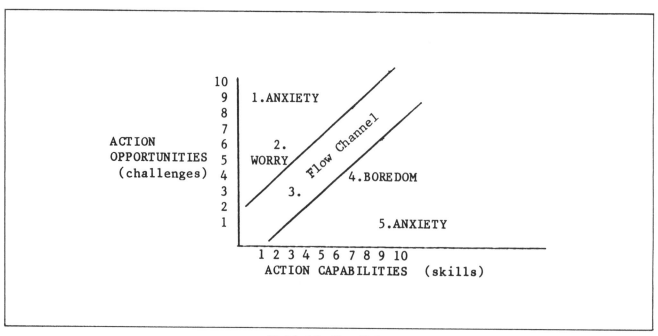

Model of the Flow State.

CHAPTER 12

FLOW AND THE RACQUETBALL EXPERIENCE

"The principle assumption in the behavioral sciences is that observable actions are the only legitimate data. As a result, inner experience has been exiled to a scientific no-man's-land. Yet the crucial focal point of psychological events is still the psyche; our thoughts and our feelings, not our objective behavior, give meaning to life. Play is a good example of this truism; here physical behavior is an unreliable guide for understanding the phenomenon. It is not so much what people do but how they perceive and interpret what they are doing that makes the activity enjoyable" (Csikszentmihalyi, p. 9).

People do care whether their actions give them enjoyment. When you enjoy what you do, your self-confidence, contentment, and feeling of closeness with others will increase. If your behavior is motivated by external pressures or desire for a reward, you may experience insecurity, frustration, and a sense of alienation. Playing racquetball provides all of these emotions.

CONTROL OF MOTIVATIONAL FORCES WHICH INFLUENCE BEHAVIOR

How can people control the forces which motivate their behavior? Flow is the answer. Poised between boredom and anxiety, flow is the complete involvement of players with their sport. The holistic sensation that people experience when they perform with positive feelings is flow. In the state of flux, action will follow action, according to an internal logic that no conscious intervention by the player can alter. You can experience this unified flow from one moment to the next. You can control your actions with little distinction between the self and your environment, stimulus and response, the past, present, or the future. A main trait of the experience is people seeking flow primar-

ily for the experience, not for the resulting extrinsic rewards.

A game such as racquetball is an obvious flow activity. Playing is the flow experience par excellence! Yet, playing the game will not guarantee you a flow experience. The flow experience can also be found in non-athletic activities. Creative efforts, including art and science, are examples. Composers and dancers describe their feelings similarly to mountain climbers or chess players. Surgeons involved in medical research and mathematicians working on the frontiers of their field responded to interviews in terms that were almost interchangeable with those used by racquetball and basketball players.

MERGER OF ACTION AND AWARENESS

Perhaps the clearest sign of flow is the merging of action with awareness. A person in flow has no dualistic perspective. The individual is aware of his/her actions, but not of the awareness itself. A racquetball player pays undivided attention to the ball and the opponent. Yet for sustained flow, one cannot reflect solely on the act of awareness. When awareness is split so that one perceives activity from "outside," flow is interrupted. Concentration upon the flow is difficult to maintain for any length of time without at least momentary interruptions. These interruptions lend themselves to racquetball perfectly.

When you have gained the requisite skill, action and awareness will merge. This sense of flow will occur only when tasks are within your ability to perform them. This merger of action and awareness is possible through a second characteristic of flow experiences: the centering of attention on a limited stimulus field, i.e., the ball. To ensure that people will concentrate on their actions, potentially intrusive stimuli must be eliminated.

MOTIVATIONAL ELEMENTS

Motivational elements are divided into several types. Competition, gain, survival and the loss of ego will be the types I shall discuss here. These factors each play an important part in motivating you. For teachers, the decision of which element to use is important! The competition and gain motivations are there from the start to finish of a match. However, survival and loss of ego can be spurious motivators, as with all types of motivation that come into play during an important match.

The simplest motivational element is competition, which insures the undivided attention of an otherwise unmotivated player. The possibility of defeat peaks the player's attention as much as prize money and trophies. Certain play activities rely on the element of physical danger to produce the centering of attention and the consciousness of flow. While racquetball does not present much physical danger, there is an element of survival present in single elminiation tournament play.

The addition of superficial motivational elements to a flow activity (competition, gain, survival) will increase your vulnerability to intrusions from "outside reality." Playing racquetball for money may increase concentration on the game. Paradoxically, the fear of loss may cause you even greater distractions. Ideally, this sense of flow is the result of your pure involvement in the game.

LOSS OF EGO

Another characteristic of the flow experience has been described by Abraham Maslow as "loss of ego." A person will become so involved in an activity that ego becomes irrelevant. Even when the sense of control (flow) comes from victory, the victory is seen as a win over personal limitations rather than over an opponent. A lot of superior racquetball players stress this notion of self-control.

Have you ever experienced the following?

"I have found myself at times when I have super concentration in a game whereby nothing else exists — nothing exists except the act of participating and swinging at the ball. The other player must be there to play the game, but I'm not concerned with him. I'm not competing with him at that point. I'm attempting to place the ball in the perfect spot, and it has no bearing on winning or losing." (Csikszentmihalyi, p. 34).

MODEL OF THE FLOW STATE

Achievement of the flow experience does not require the presence of external goals or rewards. The various elements of the flow experience are linked together and dependent upon one another. By limiting your stimulus field, the flow activity will allow you to concentrate on your actions and ignore outside distractions. This is a feeling of potential control of your environment. The flow activity also has clear and noncontradictory rules. People who perform in the flow activity temporarily forget their identity and its attendent problems. This alone makes the process intrinsically rewarding.

A flow episode may start merely by directly your awareness to meet the requirements of flow. Limit the stimulus field to allow the merging of action and awareness. Most people, however, rely on external cues to attain flow states. Flow activities then may be formed as those structured systems of action which help us to produce flow experiences.

Despite vast differences, flow activities share certain characteristics. Specifically, activities that reliably produce the flow experience are similar in that they provide active opportunities that unburden your mind. A presentation of this idea is illustrated in Diagram 12-1.

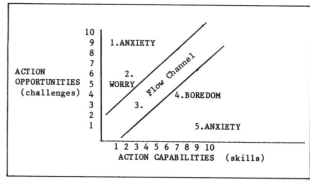

Diagram 12-1. *Model of the Flow State.*

1. When a person believes that action opportunities are too demanding for his/her capabilities, the resultant stress becomes anxiety (challenge-9, skill-1).
2. When the ratio of capabilities is higher, but the challenges are still too demanding, the resulting feeling is worry (challenge-6, skill-2).
3. The state of flow is felt when opportunities for action are in balance with the player's skills. The experience is then autotelic (challenge-3, skill-3).

4. When skills are greater than opportunities, a state of boredom results (challenge-4, skill-7).
5. Boredom again fades into anxiety when the ratio between skills and opportunities becomes too large (challenge-1, skill-9).

THE TOURNAMENT EXPERIENCE

People experience flow when they perceive opportunities for action evenly matched to their capabilities. An example of one such situation is shown in Diagram 12-2. You are the 4th seed in the open division of a racquetball tournament with 16 entries. Situation A: you play the 13th seed during the first round. Your skills are superior, and the match seems boring. Situation B: you won the first round and are playing the 5th seed in the quarter finals. The skill of your opponent is close, which permits the best opportunity to experience flow. Situation C: you won the match and are playing the number 1 seed in the semi-finals. The opponent has superior skills which induces anxiety.

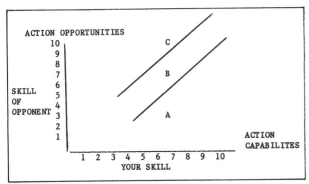

Diagram 12-2. *Example of Flow and Non flow Situations in an Open Racquetball Tournament.*

You had a greater potential for boredom in situation A, the greatest opportunity for flow in situation B, and the greatest anxiety in situation C. Each match in the tournament can be reliably rated in terms of its objective difficulties. It should be stressed that whether or not a person experiences this flow depends only in part upon the objective conditions of his environment.

REACHING AND MAINTAINING FLOW

To attain and maintain flow, you must merge your action and awareness with your focus of attention on the ball. The intrusion of secondary motivational forces, such as competition or money, may increase your concen-

tration. These same factors can also interrupt your flow through the fear of loss. You must block your ego from entering the environment in order to reach flow. You also must place the ball in a perfect spot.

Do not compete against your opponent. Neither winning or losing can affect your flow experience. Flow will not require goals or external reward, when the skill is present. When certain characteristics are present, the individual can experience control over the environment. These characteristics **ARE** linked and are necessary to sustain this flow.

"We can also be anxious or bored — anxious because there seems to be so much that could be done, bored because there is nothing one can do. It is then that flow comes into play. Flow activities are arbitrary patterns that people use to give shape to their experience. They are arbitrary because physiological needs or social constraints do not dictate their form. Flow is potentially the most creative, fulfilling kind of experience, because it is free of evolutionary and historical constraints and hence allows people to experiment with new actions and new challenges. Deep-flow activities like chess, climbing, composing, and surgery, provide structure to perception and action for long periods of time. Such activities produce vivid experience which can transform and give meaning to a person's whole life." (Csikszentmihalyi, p. 77).

LET THE FLOW BE WITH YOU!

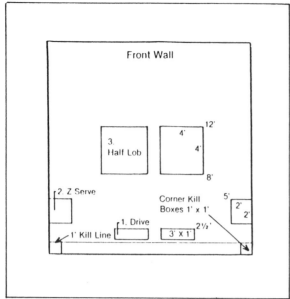

Electrical Tape Guidelines on the Front Wall.

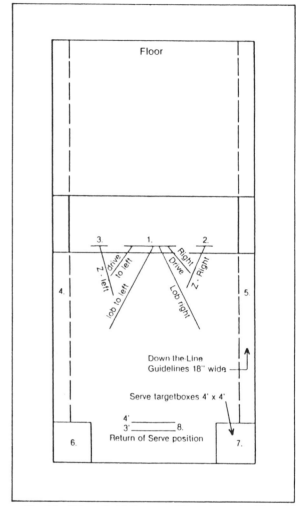

Electrical Tape Guidelines and Targets on the Floor.

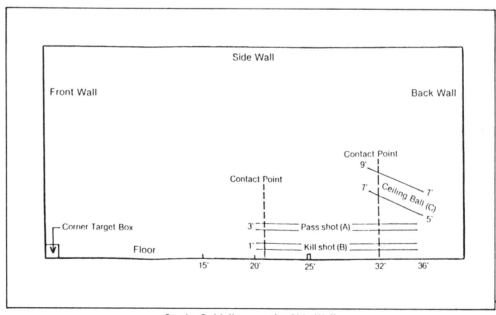

Stroke Guidelines on the Side Wall.

CHAPTER 13

TRAINING AIDS FOR RACQUETBALL

Only a few players will become exceptionally skilled athletes, readily mastering all necessary skills. Every racquetball skill is learned through differing methods at varying rates of speed. Some people naturally learn faster through individual instruction and reading books. Other players learn better through group instruction and a lot of practice. Some skills are learned more quickly through the use of training aids.

Training aids vary according to your level of ability. Some included here are the most common aids used by teaching pros, with an explanation of their purpose and a brief description. These descriptions include the use of masking tape on the court walls, the frisbee, the Yellon racquet, a nerf racquetball, a ball machine, video tape equipment and other aids.

TAPING THE RACQUETBALL COURT

The beginning racquetball player needs time to become familiar with the court environment and the various angles at which the ball caroms. It may take some players up to six months or a year to familiarize themselves with the court even if they know the game rules and have a coach working with them. Most beginners can greatly improve their skill during this initial period by playing on a court which has been taped to emphasize certain guidelines.

Few, if any, players who gaze into the racquetball court for the first time realize just how structured the game really is. They look at the helter skelter court activity and think that this chaos is the nature of racquetball but it is not chaos. First impressions will eventually be dispelled. Diagrams 13-1A,B,C; 13-2A,B,C and 13-3 of a racquetball court include the front wall, floor, and side wall, respectively. They have been marked with electrical tape to help the beginner with targets for specific shots to reveal some of the game's structure. Most clubs use a teaching court, but these may not include all the lines I have shown. In fact, they may have additional lines. The lines have been named and measured for your convenience.

Diagrams 13-1A, 13-1B, 13-1C are layouts of the front wall. The boxes which are located off the floor represent targets for the seven basic serves of racquetball. They include:
1. Drive Serve
2. Jam Serve
3. Z-Serve
4. Overhead Z-Serve
5. Half Lob Serve
6. Z-Lob Serve
7. High-Lob Serve

Using the front wall target will greatly improve the beginner's serving accuracy. If you would initiate the serve from the right spot in the service box and hit the appropriate target

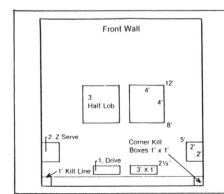
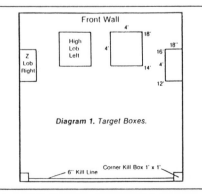
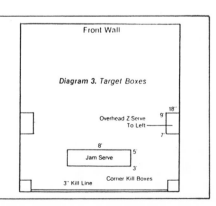

Diagram 13-1A,B,C. *Electrical Tape Guidelines on the Front Wall.*

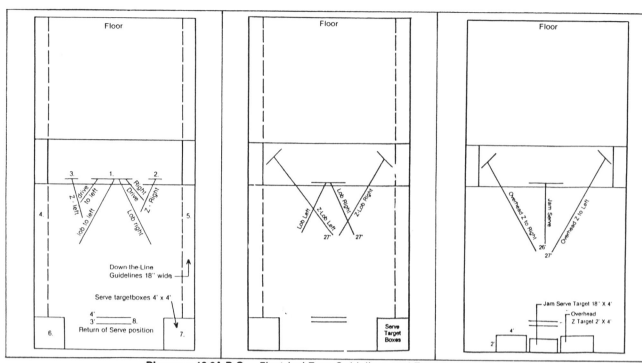

Diagrams 13-2A,B,C. *Electrical Tape Guidelines and Targets on the Floor.*

marked on the front wall, chances for a good serve are excellent. When the server hits a good serve, he/she then can shift attention to the setup position after the serve. While some serve targets may not be taught to beginners, it is good to show them that there is a lot more to learn about the game of racquetball. I would encourage beginning players to take intermediate and advanced lessons when they feel ready.

The lines connected to the floor in Diagram 13-1 represent targets for the player to use when ending the rally:

8. Corner Kill Boxes. The boxes in the corners are targets when the shooter is in front court.

9. Kill Lines. The kill lines (3" and 6") are targets for intermediates and advanced players to practice ending the rally from back court and the back wall. The 6" line should be the goal of the intermediate player, whereas the 3" line should be the goal of the advanced player. (A special note is necessary for beginners: it takes a good year of practice with proper instruction to develop the court awareness and the strokes necessary to execute a consistent kill shot during a game. Do not become discouraged!)

Diagrams 13-2A, 13-2B, 13-2C are floor plans for the racquetball court. The lines should help the beginning player learn correct positioning at the beginning of and during the rally. The lines which originate in the service box (1,2,3) represent where each serve begins and are extended to the setup position in center court after the serve. The dotted lines (4,5) which extend the length of the court form an imaginary alley which can be used to guide the ball down the lines during practice and play. You should position yourself outside the dotted line and swing your racquet inside the dotted line. This will help you develop spacial awareness between yourself, the wall, and the ball. The two boxes in the back court (6,7) represent targets for your serves. All of your serves should finish in or near these boxes. The two lines, in the center near the back wall (8), represent the return of serve position. If you are the receiver, start on these two lines, do not cheat to one side, in front of or behind this spot. A good server will ace you more frequently if you wander in back court.

The third diagram is the side wall and the tape is a guideline to help you develop the stroke mechanics for a kill shot, pass shot or a ceiling ball. Stand outside the dotted line on the floor and swing the racquet between the lines on the side wall to practice the appro-

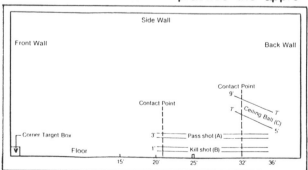

Diagram 13-3. *Stroke Guidelines on the Side Wall.*

Photo 13-1. *Set Up, Backswing & Wrist Cock.*

Photo 13-3. *Contact.*

Photo 13-2. *Arm Swing, Step, Shoulder Rotation.*

Photo 13-4. *Follow Through.*

priate shot. The horizontal dotted line on the side wall represents the contact point between the ball and the racquet. Your body must be oriented correctly to this line just prior to dropping the ball. Lastly, the player can use the 3" and 6" kill lines on the front wall as targets for his/her shots.

FRISBEE FOR THE BACKHAND

In racquetball, the backhand tends to be the most difficult shot to learn, because of its unnatural arm motion, a different grip, and the necessary body position it requires. The backhand does not usually give you as much

power as the forehand and it is easier for your opponent to cover.

An excellent teaching aid which can help you to learn backhand skill is the frisbee. The throwing motion required for a frisbee is quite similar to that of the backhand. The wrist action necessary to throw a frisbee will add power to your backhand shot. Fundamentally, by learning to throw a frisbee you will help yourself learn the motor-nurial pathways necessary to execute the correct backhand stroke. Pictures 13-1 to 13-4 demonstrate the proper motion.

Beginners should play frisbee off the court as often as possible. More importantly, practice the backhand with your racquet on the court. When you are on the court, do not tense up, but remember to relax, and think of playing frisbee in the park.

TRAINING AIDS TO IMPROVE YOUR WEAKNESSES

All players, regardless of their skill level, have relative strengths and weaknesses to their game. Intermediate players have attained a fundamental skill level, but they still have ups and downs on the racquetball court. These downs are the result of weaknesses which the good opponent can exploit on any given day.

NERF RACQUETBALL CAN BE FUN

The intermediate player should focus efforts in two areas; stroke technique and concentration. The proper stroke technique will add consistency and accuracy to your game. Yet, it is difficult to improve stroke technique while actually playing a game. You should practice your stroke off the court, by using a racquet, a nerf racquetball, and a mirror (see Picture 13-5). Find a suitable model either by watching the best player in your area, buying a well illustrated book which demonstrates good form or asking your local pro to teach you what to practice. When you know the proper techniques to practice, watch yourself in the mirror and study your form.

Utilizing a nerf racquetball with your racquet will give you a more realistic sensation of hitting the ball, and you will be able to see where the ball goes. Needless to say, your wife or mother won't be upset because the damage will be minimal. This technique can be practiced anywhere in the house with or without a mirror. You can use any object in the room as a target to practice your control. Hallways are great places for practicing your pinch shot. The nerf ball is also an excellent aid for learning how to put spin on the ball. You can experiment as much as you like because there will be little stress exerted on your arm or body. Finally, nerf racquetball is an excellent training aid for juniors. Few juniors are able to go to a court as often as their energy and enthusiasm would like. Picture 13-5 shows a nerf racquetball and a regulation racquetball. You can buy a nerf racquetball at most tennis clubs and sporting goods stores.

THE YELLON RACQUET

The Yellon Racquet gets its name from its inventor, Mike Yellon, one of the top pros in the world. To make the racquet, use an old or inexpensive racquet. Ask your pro to re-

Photo 13-5. *Practice Stroke With Nerf Ball Off Court.*

Photo 13-6. *Arrange Strings to Form Sweet Spot of Racquet.*

string this racquet with six vertical and six horizontal strings, arranged to form the sweet spot of that racquet (see Picture 13-6).

The purpose of practicing with this modified racquet is to **FORCE** you to contact the ball specifically in the sweet spot. Any ball hit that is off center will go right through the racquet. The benefit of practicing this way is to develop hand-eye coordination and gain better control of the ball. You will soon realize tremendous improvement in your ability to keep your eye on the ball. In my opinion, watching the ball all the way to the racquet is the secret to hitting winners. After practicing with the Yellon Racquet several times, play a game with it; you will be amazed at the results. Keep this racquet in your bag and use it as part of your warm-up for a match. Do not forget to switch to your normal racquet before you play, unless you're feeling invincible!

FOLLOW THE WHITE LINE

By continually trying to improve your concentration on the ball, you will become a better player. Concentration is not simply watching the ball; it is fixing your eye **ON THE BALL** so that nothing else enters your mind. Think of absolute concentration as a camera lens, focusing on a picture. When you can stop at will, much like a snap shot, you are on the way to absolute concentration.

This level of concentration is difficult to obtain, and only comes as the result of a lot of hard work. One technique which can be practiced on the court is to focus your eye on a white line which has been painted on the ball. Use "White-Out" or "Liquid Paper" to paint a white line on the seam of your racquetball (see Picture 13-7).

Photo 13-7. *White Line on the Seam of Ball.*

Begin by hitting ceiling balls and focusing your eyes on the white line, not the ball! This method will enable you to simulate a camera lens focusing on an object. Gradually, this line will become more defined in your mind's eye. If the line wobbles on an angle, bring it back to a vertical rotation with your racquet. When you have accomplished this task, you will be a long way toward seeing the ball as if it were floating through midair and controlled by you.

TECHNOLOGY IN RACQUETBALL

The previous teaching aids are useful for improving specific aspects of your game, and they then may not require any formal instruction. However, the following teaching aids (ball machine and video taping) encompass the entire game and do require professional assistance, instruction, and evaluation to maximize their effectiveness.

By all means, use a ball machine for refining and perfecting your skills; it's benefits include: precise repetition of a setup or shot to be practiced, a close replication of game conditions, and keeping you in condition. A ball machine also gives you the flexibility to practice virtually every shot in racquetball. Also, by using the ball machine, you will not wear out or bore your partner. How many times have you played a match where your opponent hits a shot in a certain way which you could not handle and you lost the match? Then, when you are on the court with a friend and you ask him/her to hit the shot the same way, they can't replicate it. How are you going to master that shot? The answer is a ball machine!

The following are a few examples of shots to practice with a ball machine:
1. The serve return — the machine will shoot drive and Z-serve at various speeds and angles with little difficulty.
2. Backwall practice — straight setups, ceiling ball setups.
3. Backwall corner practice — down-the-line crack shots or forehand and backhand, turn-around drills.
4. Offensive returns of ceiling ball setups.
5. Middle court practice — when the machine is behind you.
6. Front court retrieving practice.
7. Any return off of any rally shot, i.e. cross-court, down-the-line.

VIDEO TAPING IS A MUST

Everyone thinks that they know what they look like, and what they are doing on the racquetball court. You will be amazed when you see yourself playing on video tape. Video taping is used as a teaching aid in almost every sport, and racquetball is no exception. However, video taping can be expensive or might not be available at all. An alternative to video is charting. Charting is an objective evaluation on paper of what occurs on the racquetball court. For a complete explanation, see Chapter 15.

Viewing a video tape of your great performance is only as valuable as your objectivity allows it to be. Two people rarely assess the same play in the same way. It is sometimes easier for you to evaluate another player. Your ego can inhibit your objectivity. In other words, did you miss a shot or did your opponent hit a shot that you could not return? Ask yourself if you were in the proper position when the ball was hit. Be honest! You must ask yourself these questions as often as possible, and always be 100% truthful.

Video taping racquetball has three major functions: (1) watch yourself and look for clues which will improve your game; (2) watch top players and see how they execute specific skills; (3) watch future opponents, and look for exploitable weaknesses in their game.

Objective video tape evaluation of any racquetball game should focus on five main points. These include: court position, shot selection, stroke technique, missed shot or mishits, and quadrants of the court which indicate relative strengths and weaknesses in the overall game.

1. Court position involves four situations:
   A. The server's position after the game.
   B. The receiver's position for the serve.
   C. A player's tendency to play close to the short line or close to the back wall during the rally.
   D. A player's tendency to play off your body covering the down-the-line or away from you covering a crosscourt shot.

2. Shot selection wins or loses most games.
   A. Shot selection is limited by your ability. If you cannot execute a shot in practice, do not attempt it in a game.
   B. Pick the easiest shot to hit based on the approach shot. Make your opponent cover a well-hit ball.
   C. If your opponent is out of position, then you may hit a more difficult shot to exploit that position.

3. Stroke technique can always be improved.
   A. Few individuals develop flawless stroke techniques. There are several reasons that support this statement. First, as the game of racquetball evolves, so does the stroke technique necessary to keep up with change. Second, everyone's physical capabilities are different, so no single technique is best for everyone.
   B. Use video tapes to watch the form of top players who have body types similar to yours.
   C. Use video tape of yourself to identify flaws in your stroke which cause errors while playing.
   D. Refine your stroke technique to set up quicker, generate more power, and control your shots better.

4. Missed Shots or Missed Hits:
   A. You must practice to eliminate mistakes in your game.
   B. Decide whether mistakes are your fault or due to the superior ability of your opponent.
   C. Mishit or missed shots are very often caused by poor court position. The difference can be one step back if you get passed or skip balls in a rally; also, one step forward if you cannot retrieve the ball or retrieve a ball and give away another setup.

5. Quadrants of the court can indicate a player's relative strengths and weaknesses.
   A. The horizontal and vertical lines divide the court into four quadrants.
   B. Note a player's winning and losing shots by placing symbols on the chart which pinpoint where the shot was taken from.
   C. Patterns will emerge showing a player's successful and unsuccessful quadrants on the court.
   D. If you have charted yourself, practice in the quadrant where you make the most mistakes.
   E. If you have charted another player, select shots which put that player in the quadrant where he/she is least effective.

Casual players can certainly improve their game by using a ball machine or watching themselves on video tape. However, the serious player will not substantially improve without both of these teaching aids; they are simply an indispensable part of racquetball and their importance cannot be overstated!

The following is a racquetball shot chart. It can be used by a player or teacher as an objective evaluation of the components of their racquetball game. Place a check under the number column for each shot missed. The person tallying can make notes in the comments column. The tallied results will pinpoint specific shots which need improvement. The comments section will identify why you missed a shot.

Table 13-1: *Racquetball Shot Chart*

BEGINNERS

Serve from one position. Five attempts, record # of legal serves.

	number	comments
Drive right	_____	_____
Drive left............................	_____	_____
Z right	_____	_____
Z left	_____	_____
Half lob right........................	_____	_____
Half lob left	_____	_____

INTERMEDIATES

Serve from two positions, total five attempts, record # serves which are legal and do not come off back wall.

High lob right	_____	_____
High lob left	_____	_____
Jam right	_____	_____
Jam left.............................	_____	_____

ADVANCED

Serve from three positions, total five attempts, record # serves which are legal and do not come off back or side walls.

Overhead-Z lob right.................	_____	_____
Overhead-Z lob left	_____	_____
Medium-overhead Z right	_____	_____
Medium-overhead Z left..............	_____	_____
Hard-overhead Z right	_____	_____
Hard-overhead Z left.................	_____	_____

SHOTS

BEGINNERS

Total five attempts. Record the # of shots which pass between the player's body and the side wall.

FOREHAND

Down-the-line Pass/Kill	25' ____	35' ____	_____	_____
Crosscourt Pass/Kill	25' ____	35' ____	_____	_____

BACKHAND

Down-the-line Pass/Kill	25' ____	35' ____	_____	_____
Crosscourt Pass/Kill	25' ____	35' ____	_____	_____

INTERMEDIATES

Total five attempts. Record the # of shots which pass between the player's body and the side wall and do not skip or come off the back wall.

FOREHAND

Kill shot...........................	25' ____	35' ____	_____	_____
Pinch shot	25' ____	35' ____	_____	_____

BACKHAND

Kill shot...........................	25' ____	35' ____	_____	_____
Pinch shot	25' ____	35' ____	_____	_____

Table 13-1: *continued*

ADVANCED

Total five attempts. Record the # of shots which pass between the player's body and the side wall and do not skip or come off the back wall.

	number	comments

FOREHAND
    Wide angle or Diamond pass.......25'_____
    Splat shot.........................25'_____ 35'_____
BACKHAND
    Wide angle or Diamond pass.......25'_____
    Splat shot.........................25'_____ 35'_____

Twelve ceiling balls must be hit continuously, the setup shot does not count, when a miss occurs the rally begins again with previous count at one miss and the # made successfully.

    Ceiling balls forehand ....
    Ceiling balls backhand.................
    Side-to-side rally ....

The following shots are the best of five attempts.

Overhead down-the-line off ceiling ball setup..........................
Kill shot off ceiling ball.....................FH ....BH
Around-the-wall ball off ceiling ball ....FH ....BH
Down-the-line off around-the-wall ball ....FH ....BH

BACK WALL
    Straight kill.........................FH ....BH
    Down-the-line pass/kill...............FH ....BH
    Crosscourt pass.....................FH ....BH
    Pinch shot ....FH ....BH

CENTER COURT
    Beginners should be setup by the tester.
    Intermediates should be setup and play the shot off one bounce.
    Advanced players should setup and play the ball out of midair.

Front wall setup
    Forehand to left corner .... right corner.......
    Backhand to left corner................. right corner.......
Front-side wall setup
    Forehand to........................... right corner.......
    Backhand to left corner.................

Front-wall-to-back-wall-rally kill ....FH ....BH
Back-wall-to-front-wall-volley kill ....FH ....BH
Wrist Drop
    Forehand.........................25'
    Backhand ....25'
Pinch rally (10 continuous)..................25' ....35'
Kill and close drill.....................FH ....BH
Turnaround drill from left corner ....right corner

CHAPTER 14

MAKE THE MOST OF YOUR COURT TIME — PRACTICE!

Improving your racquetball game at every skill level will require a lot of practice. Racquetball, like any other sport, requires practice of the fundamentals, whether it is blocking in football or in the pirouette in ballet. Practice is necessary if you expect to be successful. To improve your skills, devote at least one hour per week to structured practice on the court. Professionals require more practice time than playing time because they receive enough playing from tournament to tournament. These hours of practice per week are necessary for the professional to keep every skill uniformly sharp. Practice is also needed to add shots, improve certain aspects of the game, and to iron out common errors. Practice improves your self-confidence and concentration.

Adopt an attitude of self-improvement and this attitude will help you to grow and develop. For example, after each game (win or lose) ask yourself, "What shot should I improve for the next time?" "Why do I find myself out of position?" Answer yourself or ask someone else how to give you an honest account of your game.

Develop a purpose in your mind while you play or practice. To improve your pinch shot, attempt to hit one at every opportunity. Forget about the score, forget about winning and losing. By playing or practicing with a purpose you will improve your racquetball skills, add to your self-confidence, and ultimately show positive results in the win column.

There are many ways to practice: practice with a partner, using two-person drills or while playing under game conditions, or practice alone by repeating one shot over and over again. Use either of these methods at different times, depending on your needs.

The following format is a system for practicing many of the important aspects of racquetball in a single hour. Every player needs to master specific shots with consistent repetition; this system will improve your game.

Players at all levels should differentiate between the levels of difficulty in the following manner. Beginners and intermediates should emphasize stationary drills (drop & hit).

The beginner should practice all shots by letting the ball bounce once before making contact. This will develop control and timing, improve your stroke mechanics, and aid eye-hand coordination. The intermediate player should practice most of the shots by hitting the ball in midair (without a bounce). This speeds up your swing, adds velocity to the ball, quickens the reflexes, and better simulates actual game conditions. The next level of difficulty is dynamic movement drills. Beginners and intermediates should perform these setup drills on one bounce (rally), whereas advanced players should practice without a bounce (volley). The final level includes game situation drills. Intermediate and advanced players should practice alone and with a partner. They should use these drills to create game situations (i.e., ceiling ball rally, serve, and return of serve).

To make your practice time most efficient, divide the court into the areas where most shots occur during a game. Diagram 14-1 identifies six positions from which different shots should be practiced. Beginners should practice from positions #1 to #6 until they attain an 80% rate of success prior to moving to the

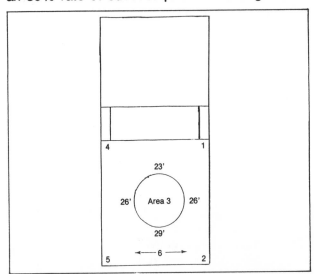

Diagram 14-1. *Six Practice Positions for Different Shots.*

intermediate techniques. This same success rate is also necessary for intermediate players who wish to move into the advanced level.

WARNING! Without proper stroke mechanics and consistency, practicing at a more difficult skill level will be a waste of your time. You will only be negatively reinforcing the flaws in your game. Be honest with yourself; this is the best policy here.

Players at all skill levels should begin every practice hour with a series of warm-up exercises which includes stretching, light ball throwing followed by gradually-harder ball throwing and finally, free form racquet swinging, both forehand and backhand.

FOREHAND AND BACKHAND SWING

A. Position #1 is 5 ft. from the short line and is used by the right-hand player for the Forehand Straight Kill-Pass Shot, Pinch Shot, and Crosscourt-Diamond Pass Shot. Position #2 is 1 ft. from the back wall and is used for the Straight Kill-Pass Shot, Splat Shot and Crosscourt Pass-Kill Shot. Position #4 is 5 ft. from the short line and is used by right-handed players for the Backhand Straight Kill-Pass Shot Pinch Shot and Crosscourt-Diamond Pass Shot. Position #5 is 1 ft. from the back wall and is used for the Straight Kill-Pass Shot, Splat Shot and Crosscourt Pass-Kill Shot. Position #3 is 7 ft. from the short line and is used for both the Forehand and Backhand practice of the Pinch Shot, Down the Line Kill-Pass Shot and Crosscourt Kill-Pass Shot.

B. During actual play, 80% to 90% of all shots will occur from these positions.

C. Positions #1, #3 and #4 occur most frequently as the retrieve of the return of serve or during the rally.

D. Positions #2 and #5 occur most frequently as the return of serve.

E. While practicing, try to develop a rhythm along with accuracy.

FRONT COURT VOLLEY

A. The opportunity to play the racquetball in midair from front court occurs more often then you might think. About two-thirds of all shots can be retrieved from center court (position #3) and about one-half of those can be played in midair.

B. Because you already have obtained center court position, and your opponent is behind you, cutting the ball off, (i.e. taking it out

of midair or on one bounce) you have a distinct advantage.

C. In the front court volley, you hit the ball to the front wall at a height of 3 to 8 ft.; you must then cut the ball off in midair taking a forehand shot to the forehand corner, or a backhand shot to the backhand corner. Position #3 can also be used to practice cutting the ball off by going down the line or crosscourt with the ball.

D. Practice your short volley from two different positions on the court. Position #6 is 10 ft. from the side wall and 3 ft. from the back wall. From position #6, the right hand player begins by rallying the ball into the right side wall, then volleys the ball for several repetitions. From the volley, the ball should be redirected into the forehand rear corner. From position #6 the right-handed player should rally the ball into the left side wall progressing into a volley, and then redirect the ball with a backhand shot into the left rear corner.

E. Practicing the short volley will help you in several ways. First, when your opponent(s) are warming up, you can practice from position #6 without interference. Second, these drills are excellent practice for doubles. Third, they are also excellent practice when you are in a confined area.

BACK WALL AND CORNER PLAY

A. Back wall play should only be used when you cannot cut the ball off in midair from front court.

1. Toss the ball off the back wall (positions #2, #5) and practice Straight Kills, Pinch Shots, Down-the-Line and Crosscourt Passes.

B. Corner play should be practiced from two points of view: the return of serve and during the rally.

1. For the return of serve, toss the ball into the backhand corner, and use a backhand return to practice the Straight Kill, Pinch Shots, Down-the-Line, and Crosscourt Passes. Repeat this process with the forehand stroke in the forehand corner.

2. To practice the corners to benefit your play during the rally, you should toss the ball into the corners, side wall first, and employ the turn around method to retrieve the shot, (i.e., toss in the backhand corner and use a forehand shot). Practice shots into the right front corner (Pinch), Crosscourt for the forehand pass and the left front corner (Pinch).

THE CEILING GAME

A. Practice ceiling ball rallies with the forehand, keeping the ball along the right sidewall, ten balls without a miss. Repeat this process with the backhand, keeping the ball along the left sidewall.

B. Practice rallying ceiling balls backhand to forehand and forehand to backhand.

C. Any ceiling ball which falls short (36' to front wall) or goes long off the back wall should be shot for a kill or pinch, forehand to forehand corner and backhand to backhand corner.

Table 14-1, is a summary of the shots you should practice from the different positions as described in this chapter. In addition, a number of repetitions is recommended for each shot. One practice session each week will keep every aspect of your game sharp. This table can be used as a model for your pre-match warmup. Good Luck! Practice to be a winner and practice to stay a winner!

Table 14-1: *Practice Hour — Shot Chart.*

PRACTICE HOUR — SHOT CHART

SHOT	POSITION-/ Repetitions	SHOT	POSITION-/ Repetitions
Straight Kill-Pass	1/10	Volley Crosscourt - BH	3/5
Crosscourt-Diamond Pass	1/10	Forehand Volley Redirect	6/5
Pinch	1/10	Backhand Volley Redirect	6/5
Straight Kill-Pass	2/10	Back Wall Kill	2/5
Crosscourt Kill-Pass	2/10	Pinch	5/5
Splat	2/10	Down-the-Line Pass	2/5
Straight Kill-Pass	4/10	Crosscourt Pass	2/5
Crosscourt-Diamond Pass	5/10	Back Wall Kill	5/5
Pinch	5/10	Pinch	5/5
Straight Kill-Pass	5/10	Down-the-Line Pass	5/5
Crosscourt Kill-Pass	5/10	Crosscourt Pass	5/5
Splat	5/10	Backhand-Corner Turnaround	5/5
Forehand-Pinch	3/10	Pinch	5/5
Down-the-Line Kill-Pass	3/10	Crosscourt	5/5
Crosscourt Kill-Pass	3/10	Down-the-Line Pass	5/5
Backhand Pinch	3/10	Forehand-Corner Turnaround	2/5
Down-the-Line Kill-Pass	3/10	Pinch	2/5
Crosscourt Kill-Pass	3/10	Crosscourt	2/5
Midair Volley-Forehand	3/10	Forehand Ceiling Ball	2/10
Midair Volley-Backhand	3/10	Backhand Ceiling Ball	5/10
Volley Down-the-Line FH	3/5	Crosscourt Ceiling Ball Rally	2/5 FH
Volley Down-the-Line BH	3/5	Crosscourt Ceiling Ball Rally	5/5 BH
Volley Crosscourt - FH	3/5		

HOW TO CHANGE YOUR GAME

Most players have difficulty changing, correcting, and/or adding new techniques to their game. The degree to which you can adapt, be flexible, and intuitively correct mistakes in your game is directly related to your ability. Your adaptability is what will finally decide the skill level at which you peak. The theory of evolution also applies to racquetball. Correcting stroke techniques, adding new shots, improving weaknesses, and practicing errors out of your game is essential for you to evolve into a better player. Do not think you are above these natural laws. The following procedure should be used to facilitate any change you desire.

OFF THE COURT

1. Study a written description of what you wish to change.
2. Mentally practice this skill correctly, and see yourself performing it on the court.
3. Break this skill down into its component parts. Feel the specific muscles which contract, and mentally cause your muscles to move entirely in the correct sequence.
4. Practice this skill without the ball in front of a mirror. Watch yourself closely! Sometimes a nerf ball can be used if you need to feel the sensation of contact.

ON THE COURT

1. Practice this skill from the stationary position using either one bounce or no bounce at all.
2. Practice this skill with a dynamic movement drill, (i.e. setup off the front wall, back wall, or ceiling.)
3. Practice this skill against a weaker opponent. Focus on the change and correct execution at the proper time. Do not worry about the score.

These practice steps should help you to improve every aspect of your game in a brief period of time without too much frustration.

SPECIALIZED PRACTICE

The following drills are one hour practice sessions for each phase of the game. As needed for improvement of your major weaknesses, they provide guidelines and a normal progression for improvement. The touring professional repeats each of these practice sessions during a one-to-two week period to keep skills sharp. As needed, you should practice

these drills from the forehand and backhand sides of the court.

The serve is the most important part of your game. The player with the most effective serve usually wins the match. Chapters 1 to 5 should be reviewed when practicing the serve.

RETURN OF SERVE

1. All good serves should be returned to the ceiling.
2. Short hop lob serves should be returned down-the-line.
3. Drive serves — if they hit the side wall, they should be killed cross corner. If they come off the back wall, kill down-the-line, crosscourt, and pinch.
4. Z serves — if they are slow, cut off and hit down-the-line & crosscourt pass shots. If they are hard and shallow, let the ball hit the side wall and pinch the return.
5. Jam serves — if they are away from your body, let them go to the back wall and shoot the return down-the-line.
6. Overhead Z — if it comes off the back wall, kill the return.

BACK WALL AND CORNERS

1. Toss the ball straight into the back wall, kill straight on one bounce or no bounce to a 3" target line on the front wall.
   A. Back wall - corner.
   B. Back wall - pinch.
   C. Back wall - crosscourt.
2. Toss the ball into the side wall — back wall corners, kill straight on one bounce or no bounce to a 3" target on the front wall.
   A. Side-back wall corner - crosscourt.
   B. Side-back wall corner - down-the-line pass.
   C. Side-back wall corner - pinch.
3. Toss the ball into the back wall — side wall corners, kill straight on one bounce or no bounce to a 3" target on the front wall.
   A. Back-side wall corner - crosscourt.
   B. Back-side wall corner - down-the-line pass.
   C. Back-side wall corner - pinch.
4. Ceiling ball setup off back wall, shoot straight crosscourt, and pinch kill shots.
5. Toss the ball into the side-back wall corner and use a forehand or backhand turnaround technique to shoot the ball down-the-line and crosscourt.
6. Hit a back wall setup off the front wall and shoot a straight kill shot.

FRONT COURT AND BACK WALL

1. There is a similarity in the low-quick stroke technique required for successful front court and back wall play. Therefore, a combination of drills in these areas is strongly recommended:
2. Aim for front wall corners to end a rally.
3. Wrist drop drill, forehand and backhand.
4. Front wall continuous rally drill.
5. Front wall rally kill drill.
6. Back wall continuous volley kill drill.
7. Kill and close drill.
8. Pinch and rekill down-the-line.
9. Volley hard from the front wall and kill the ball down-the-line, crosscourt, cross corner, and same corner.
10. Front wall — back wall setup, kill down-the-line from front court.

MIDCOURT

1. Practice in the 22' to 29' zone past the short line.
2. Practice setups off the front wall and front-side wall with a bounce and no bounce.
   A. Down-the-line
   B. Crosscourt kill
   C. Corner kill
   D. Pinch
3. Around-the-wall ball setup — cut off in mid-air and kill the ball.
4. Blind reaction drill with partner.
5. Kill and close drill.
6. Continuous rally control drill — hit the ball to the front wall while first moving backward (15' to 30'), then forward 30' to 15').

CEILING BALL

1. Rally 100 ceiling balls to the forehand, kill the bad ones, and repeat with backhand.
2. Rally a ceiling ball to the forehand, then crosscourt to the backhand, then down-the-line to the backhand, and crosscourt to the forehand again. Do this continuously 20 times. Kill bad ceiling balls.
3. Rally ceiling balls crosscourt, forehand to backhand to forehand to backhand. Kill bad ceiling balls.
4. Play a ceiling ball game with a partner.

OVERHEADS

1. Throw a ball overhand from 36' to a 6" front wall target.
   A. down-the-line
   B. crosscourt
   C. cross corner
2. Toss a ball overhead and shoot overheads from 36' to a 6" front wall target.
   A. down-the-line
   B. crosscourt
   C. cross corner
3. Hit ceiling ball setups to your forehand. If they are short, shoot a straight kill; if they are long, kill off the backwall, and, if it is good, shoot an overhead. Repeat this with backhand ceiling ball setups and forehand overhead shots.

PINCH AND SPLAT

1. Continuous pinch rally from 25'.
2. Continuous wide angle pinch rally from 35'.
3. Setup off the front wall and pinch from mid-court.
4. Setup ceiling ball off back wall and pinch.
5. Drop and splat from 25' and 35' without a bounce.
6. Ceiling ball setup (close to side wall), splat the ball.
7. Back wall setup (close to side wall), splat the ball.

PARTNER DRILLS

1. Back wall continuous volley kill drill.
2. Blind reaction drill from midcourt.
3. Ceiling ball game.
4. Return of serve practice.
5. Serve practice.
6. Front court continuous crosscourt rally.
7. Front court continuous rally down-the-line then crosscourt.
8. Ball into back wall — front court volley kill drill.
9. Down-the-line rally kill drill.

```
[------------------------------------------------------------------]
]                                                                  1
1                                                                  1
1                                                                  1
1                                                                  J
1                                                                  1
1                                                                  1
1                                                                  1
1                                                                  1
1                                                                  1
1                                                                  1
1                                                                  1
1                                                                  1
1                                                                  1
4                                                                  1
[------------------------------------------------------------------]
1                     DF: :                                        1
1                     LB: : :                                      1
1                          : : : . .                              1
1                     DB: : : : : :                                1
[------------------------------------------------------------------]
1                                                                  1
1                                                                  1
1                                                                  1
1                                                                  1
1                                                                  1
1                                                                  1
1                                                                  1
1                                                                  1
1                                                                  1
1                                                                  1
1                                                                  1
1 CCPa: : : :                                                      1
1 DLPa: : .                                                        1
1 CB: : :                                                          1
1 CCE: : .                                                         1
1 K . . .                                             CCPa: : 1
[------------------------------------------------------------------]
                         BACK WALL
```

Charting the Serve — Normal Scoring.

CHAPTER 15

WIN MORE THROUGH CHARTING

Once upon a time, a great man-bird, The Gar, swooped down on me from Mount Buffalo. He was impressive with his 6'6" frame, and foretold a great revelation to this plebeian. "Lou," he said, "chart your opponent's racquetball game. Study the picture it forms, and you will defeat him."

Well! To say the least, I was awe-struck! What did the Gar mean? He said, "Scout and record your opponent's strengths and weaknesses. With the information, you can prepare a game plan that will eventually help you to defeat the player you have scouted." (Garfinkel, 1982, p. 28). In addition, having someone chart you will point out the strengths and weaknesses in your own game.

Faults are sometimes difficult to recognize or to admit. The chart, however, does not lie! The picture it can give you can help you win games. This chapter will detail how you can chart the end of every rally, and the serve. Beginners, intermediates, and advanced players can be taught to read, interpret, plan, and execute chart information in order to improve their games. The model charting source was **THE GAR CHART,** developed by Charlie Garfinkel, holder of many national titles.

Before I proceed into the body of this chapter, you should understand that charting is a complex and difficult task. After you initially familiarize yourself with the symbols and basic charting techniques, you can use your own method to personalize your charts. Determine what information you specifically need to know, then alter the technique to personalize that information. Make your chart to your strengths and weaknesses. You will then have a good mental picture of what happens in your game.

For example, the chart will show which shots skipped to end a rally. Perhaps, of more importance is what shot caused the skip to occur. (Note that in Diagram 15-1, shots 15 FK, FK, 9 FK, were skips from back wall ceiling balls.) Remember, be creative, flexible, and discover new ways for charting to help improve your game.

CHARTING THE END OF EVERY RALLY

Charting the end of every rally will show exactly what you do on the court. The numbers on the chart represent where the winning shot was taken and the number of points scored; i.e., the first point, 1 FK, was a skip ball from the right rear corner (Diagram 15-1). A side out has no number notation (B Splat).

The notation circled 17 FK is the seventeenth point scored by Obremski on a skip ball from Brannan. Winners appear as 13 FK or 11A. Misses by the opponent appear as 18 OHK. Personal misses are on the opponent's chart (see Diagram 15-1A - FRPi). In other words, Diagram 15-1A shows all Dan Obremski's points — his good shots and Dan Brannon's errors.

Forehand and backhand shots are denoted by F and B. They should be the first notation following a number and after the direction or shot., i.e., 16BPi or FCCPI. Direction notations follow; i.e., 7BCCP: the seventh point scored on a backhand crosscourt passing shot. No given direction indicates a straight shot; i.e., 5BK is the fifth point on a backhand straight kill. Last in the sequence is the specific shot taken. FRPi is a forehand reverse pinch. This system may seem complicated. A little practice and common sense, however, will bring about the reward. You will play better racquetball and win more matches.

CHARTING THE SERVE

Do not underestimate the importance of charting the serve and return. At advanced levels, these charts may mean the difference between victory or defeat. If you can chart an advanced player some time, you will learn the combination of serves used in a series to deceive the receiver. You can watch the execution of the same serve from different positions in the service box. Make a mental note of what serve returns are most effective against which serves. Then you can prepare yourself to execute those returns when you play this opponent.

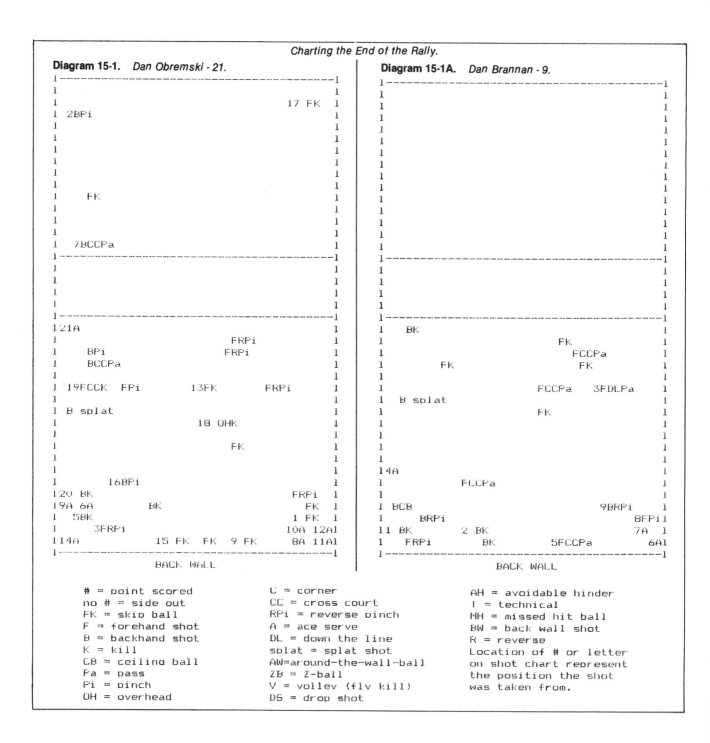

Charting the End of the Rally.

Diagram 15-1. *Dan Obremski - 21.*

Diagram 15-1A. *Dan Brannan - 9.*

```
# = point scored           C = corner                AH = avoidable hinder
no # = side out            CC = cross court          I = technical
FK = skip ball             RPi = reverse pinch       MH = missed hit ball
F = forehand shot          A = ace serve             BW = back wall shot
B = backhand shot          DL = down the line        R = reverse
K = kill                   splat = splat shot        Location of # or letter
CB = ceiling ball          AW=around-the-wall-ball   on shot chart represent
Pa = pass                  ZB = Z-ball               the position the shot
Pi = pinch                 V = volley (fly kill)     was taken from.
OH = overhead              DS = drop shot
```

Charting the serve requires a stream-lined technique (Diagrams 15-2 & 15-2A). First, fix the position of the serve with the serve number. Do not write the serve down yet. Then fix the position of the return. Write down the return and what followed: i.e., skip, kill, rekill, rally. Now write in the serve. Do not watch the rally until you have charted everything.

Ninety-five percent of serve returns will come from the side served to; i.e., backhand return from backhand side of the court. Because of the consistency, F or B is unnecessary next to the serve return on the chart unless some-

thing unusual occurs. This technique will save you time and attention. If you miss something, don't panic; simply proceed to the next serve.

Diagrams 15-2 & 15-2A chart the serve with a different scoring system, a point scored after every rally. This can be misleading the first time you chart a serve using a normal scoring system. The server will probably stand in the same spot hitting the same two serves 50 times during the game.

One method of charting is to record only different serves. A symbol for frequency can be added, i.e., placing a period next to the symbol

Diagram 15-2. *Marcy - 21.*

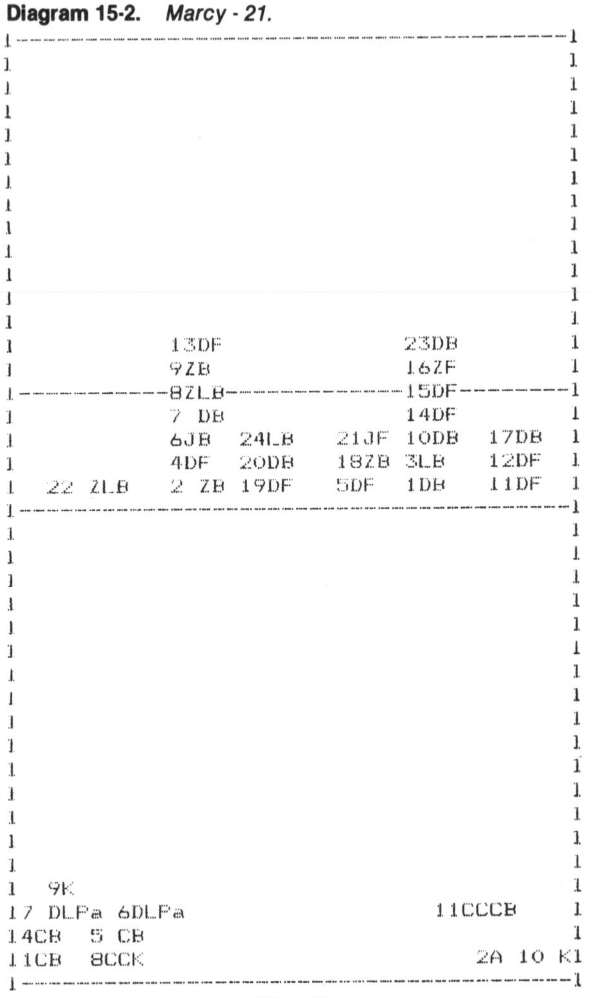

```
|--------------------------------------------|
|                                            |
|                                            |
|                                            |
|                                            |
|                                            |
|                                            |
|                                            |
|                                            |
|                                            |
|                                            |
|         13DF            23DB               |
|         9ZB             16ZF               |
|-------8ZLB----------------15DF---------|
|         7 DB            14DF               |
|        6JB   24LB   21JF 10DB   17DB       |
|        4DF   20DB   18ZB 3LB    12DF       |
|  22 ZLB  2 ZB 19DF   5DF   1DB  11DF       |
|--------------------------------------------|
|                                            |
|                                            |
|                                            |
|                                            |
|                                            |
|                                            |
|                                            |
|                                            |
| 9K                                         |
| 17 DLPa 6DLPa              11CCCB          |
| 14CB   5 CB                                |
| 11CB   8CCK                2A 10 K1        |
|--------------------------------------------|
                  BACK WALL
```

Diagram 15-2A. *Marilyn - 8.*

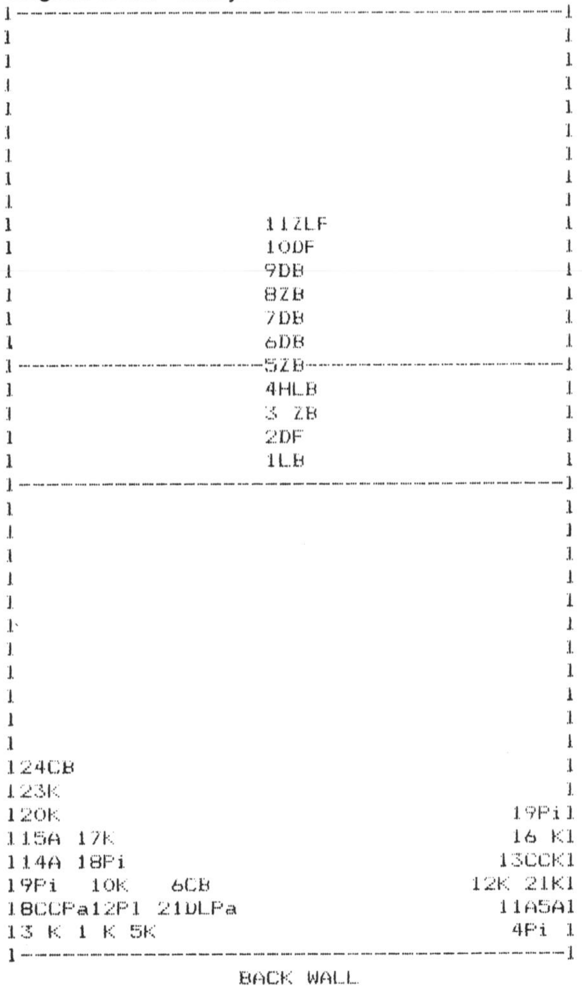

```
|--------------------------------------------|
|                                            |
|                                            |
|                                            |
|                                            |
|                                            |
|                                            |
|              11ZLF                         |
|              10DF                          |
|              9DB                           |
|              8ZB                           |
|              7DB                           |
|              6DB                           |
|--------------5ZB-----------------------|
|              4HLB                          |
|              3 ZB                          |
|              2DF                           |
|              1LB                           |
|--------------------------------------------|
|                                            |
|                                            |
|                                            |
|                                            |
|                                            |
|                                            |
|                                            |
| 24CB                                       |
| 23K                                        |
| 20K                              19Pi      |
| 15A 17K                          16 K      |
| 14A 18Pi                         13CCK     |
| 9Pi  10K    6CB                  12K 21K   |
| 18CCPa12P1 21DLPa                11A5A1    |
| 13 K 1 K 5K                      4Pi       |
|--------------------------------------------|
                  BACK WALL
```

Charting the serve uses the same symbols as charting the end of the rally. In addition, new symbols are needed to identify various serves.

D = Drive serve
Z = Z serve
J = Jam serve
L = Lob serve
HL = Half lob serve
ZL = Z-Lob serve

The # preceeding the serve 1DB indicates the position of the server in the service box. The letter after the serve B or F indicates the side of the court the serve went according to the hand or the server. A serve which is circled is an illegal serve, i.e. 7DB – short serve. The serve which follows numerically is the second serve 8ZLB. Every serve must have a return of serve with the same #.

i.e. 1DB =1CB. F or B are not needed unless the receiver does opposite of what was expected. Location of the notations and the symbols used have the same meaning as the rally. However, several notations are necessary:
6DLPa = good return of serve, rally follows.
3K =skip ball by receiver
17K = side out
4Pi = rekill of return

notation, DB::::. means 21 drives serves to the backhand (see Diagram 15-2B). A similar modification should be used for the serve return.

Notation for the result could be placed adjacent to or outside the court diagram; i.e., O K... means three backhand kill attempts by the receiver — one was rekilled by the server, one skipped, and one was a winner. Of course, this system will not show which return corresponds to each serve. If that information is important to you, modify the technique to suit yourself.

A TEACHING AID

The teaching pro can show his students the many benefits of charting. Teaching racquetball via visual aids, especially video taping, is also an excellent method. Charting could possibly be the next best thing. A coach should

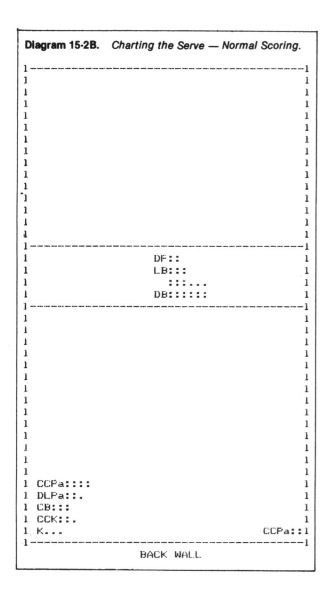

Diagram 15-2B. *Charting the Serve — Normal Scoring.*

```
1---------------------------------------1
1                                       1
1                                       1
1                                       1
1                                       1
1                                       1
1                                       1
1                                       1
1                                       1
1                                       1
1                                       1
·1                                      1
1                                       1
1                                       1
1                                       1
1----------------------------------------1
1              DF::                     1
1              LB:::                    1
1                 ::::...               1
1              DB::::::                 1
1---------------------------------------1
1                                       1
1                                       1
1                                       1
1                                       1
1                                       1
1                                       1
1                                       1
1                                       1
1                                       1
1                                       1
1                                       1
1                                       1
1 CCPa::::                              1
1 DLPa::.                               1
1 CB:::                                 1
1 CCK::.                                1
1 K...                        CCPa::1
1---------------------------------------1
              BACK WALL
```

supplement verbal instructions through the use of pictures; students will then better understand exactly what you're trying to show them.

The coach's next step should be to have students critique one another while learning to read these charts. The student will then be better able to formulate a game-winning strategy.

Each player has strengths and weaknesses in his/her game. Your goal as a coach should be to identify these weaknesses, and then formulate a game plan to exploit the weaknesses. A word of caution: don't use the same play continually, even if it is successful. Remember, your opponent also has the ability to adjust and you might lose the advantage if he figures out how to beat your strength.

THE SERVE AND SERVE RETURN

Interpretation of the serve and the serve return are easy, since you begin from the stationary position. Observe which serves your opponent hits best, and which side of the court he prefers. What receiving position can you take to anticipate this serve? Which serve return best neutralizes this serve?

The service chart should identify the receiver's weaker side of the court (forehand or backhand) on the serve return. Do not assume this will be the same for every rally. Which serves (drive, Z, lob) gave the receiver the most trouble? When the receiver hit an accurate return, which position on the court best covered that return?

THE RALLY

Interpretation of the rally requires a more in-depth understanding of charts than does serve interpretation. Everything occurs from dynamic movements which will require your judgment as a chart-maker. First, draw a line down the center of the chart from the service box to the back wall. This divides the court into a left half and right half, which identifies the weaker half. Then draw a horizontal line across the chart 30' from the front wall. Observe whether the player was less effective in front of or behind the 30' line (midcourt, back court).

Add this information to what you already have charted about the forehand or backhand weaknesses of your opponent. Now you have a quadrant to attack; i.e., left front, right front, left rear, and right rear. Draw the center and horizontal lines on several charts in this chapter. Identify the weakness, and formulate a plan of attack to include; what serves to use, and which quadrant(s) to exploit with the serve return and during the rally.

BEGINNERS: IMPROVE YOUR GAME

Beginning players should have their game charted to help them recognize its glaring weaknesses. The chart will depict your obvious errors, faults you cannot pick up on while the game is in progress. Typically, beginners will lag in back court and wait to see where the opponent hits the ball. Many mishit balls occur because the beginner is unprepared. The rallies

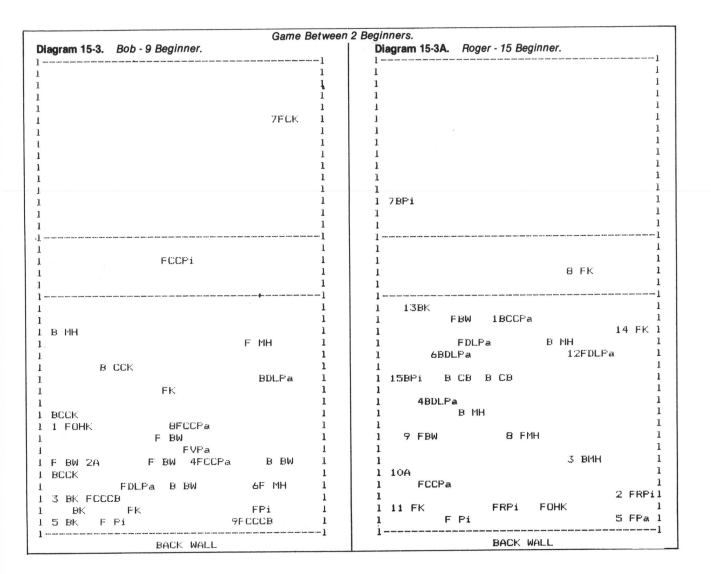

Diagram 15-3. *Bob - 9 Beginner.*

Diagram 15-3A. *Roger - 15 Beginner.*

are often long, because the ball is hit high, and usually ends on a miss or massive skip (a ball which comes off the racquet straight down into the floor).

Diagrams 15-3 & 15-3A show a game between two beginners. Observe on Diagram 15-3 how deeply Bob played his shots. The majority of forehand shots were taken from the left rear quadrant. Examine Diagram 15-3A to count the number of errors. Diagram 15-3A demonstrates better center court position. However, a large number of forehand shots were made (Diagram 15-3A) and missed (Diagram 15-3) from the backhand. Roger also hit many shots off the back wall which never reached the front wall.

INTERMEDIATES: EXPLOIT THE WEAKNESS

Intermediate players should chart both themselves and their opponents. Once again, charting will reveal the weaknesses in both players' games. The intermediate player will already have some mastery of stroke mechanics, several shot selections, comprehension of basic game concepts, and a good awareness of center court position. Typically though, intermediates have weak backhands, or they run too far forward and are easily passed. Charting the opponent will easily reveal these weaknesses to you. You can then form a game plan to take advantage of this knowledge.

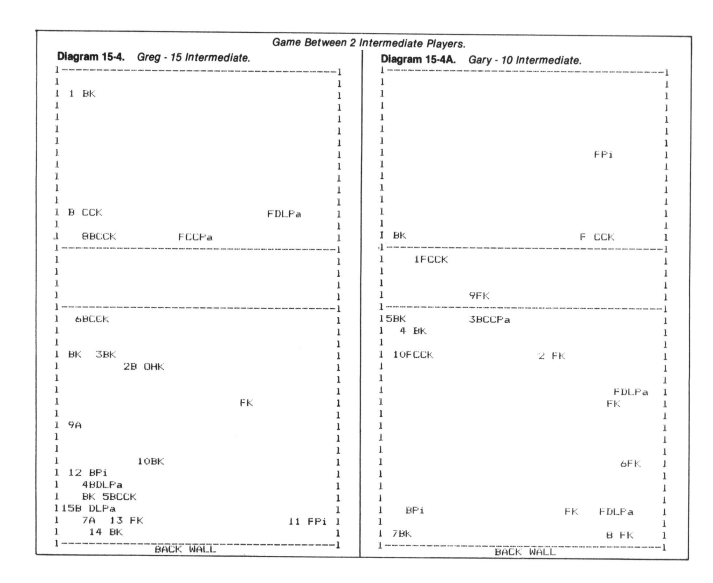

Diagram 15-4. *Greg - 15 Intermediate.*

Diagram 15-4A. *Gary - 10 Intermediate.*

Diagrams 15-4 & 15-4A depicts a game between two intermediate players. Observe how Greg scored all but one point from the backhand side. Both Greg and Gary were playing the ball to the backhand side of the court, to Greg's advantage.

Gary scored well with his forehand. He had four errors by Greg's forehand. Greg, playing close to the front wall, converted several of Gary's kills from the front court. Gary could have won by stategically playing Greg's forehand more and hitting more pass shots.

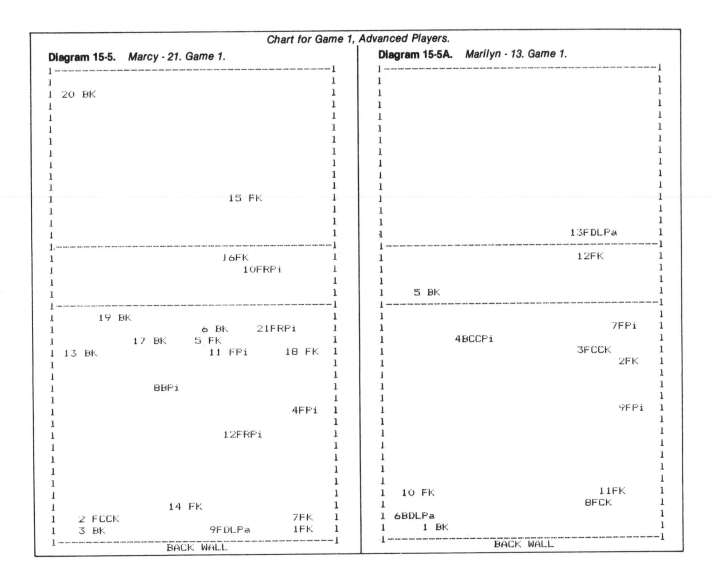

Diagram 15-5. *Marcy - 21. Game 1.*

Diagram 15-5A. *Marilyn - 13. Game 1.*

CHART AND WIN

The following is a three-game match between two advanced female players. The games were 21 points, with a point awarded after every rally. Marcy had previously observed Marilyn, noting that she charges the front court to kill the ball. Marcy's game plan was to keep Marilyn in back court with passing shots.

Diagrams 15-5 & 15-5A are the chart for the first game. Marcy caught Marilyn running into the front court. Marcy's passes were jamming Marilyn due to Marilyn's offensive style of play. Marcy won the game easily, 21-13. Marilyn, however, hit a group of forehand winners from the right front area, neutralizing Marcy's crosscourt passes (15-5A).

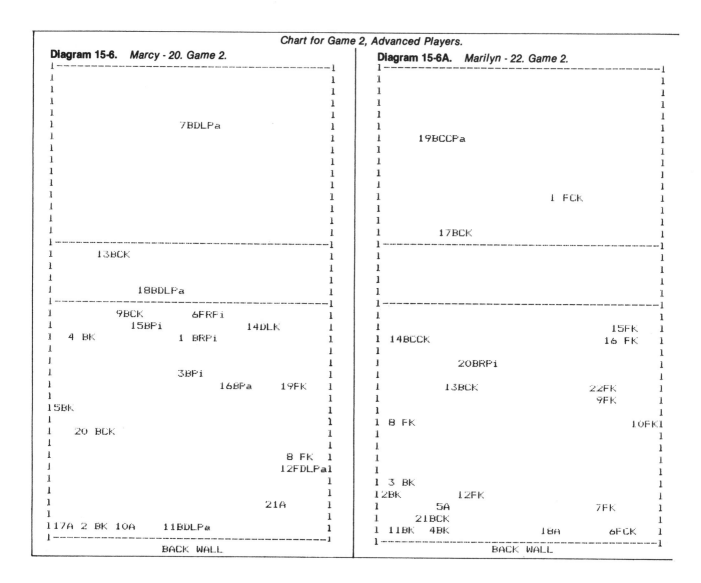

Diagram 15-6. *Marcy - 20. Game 2.*

Diagram 15-6A. *Marilyn - 22. Game 2.*

BACK WALL

Diagrams 15-6 & 15-6A are the chart for game two. Marcy used the same strategy, but Marilyn won the game, 22-20. Marilyn adjusted her court position in this game to cover Marcy's pass shots. Marilyn dropped back deeper and closer to the side wall after her serve. This enabled her to cut off Marcy's passes with pinch shots. Marcy attempted better passing shots in this game. She then pressed, giving up many back wall setups which Marilyn killed (shots 2, 4, 6, 7, 11, & 21).

Diagrams 15-7 & 15-7A show the tie breaker. Marcy changed her strategy. She exploited Marilyn's deeper position by hitting virtually all kill shots. This strategy, coupled with Marilyn's high risk offense, gave Marcy the victory, 21-18.

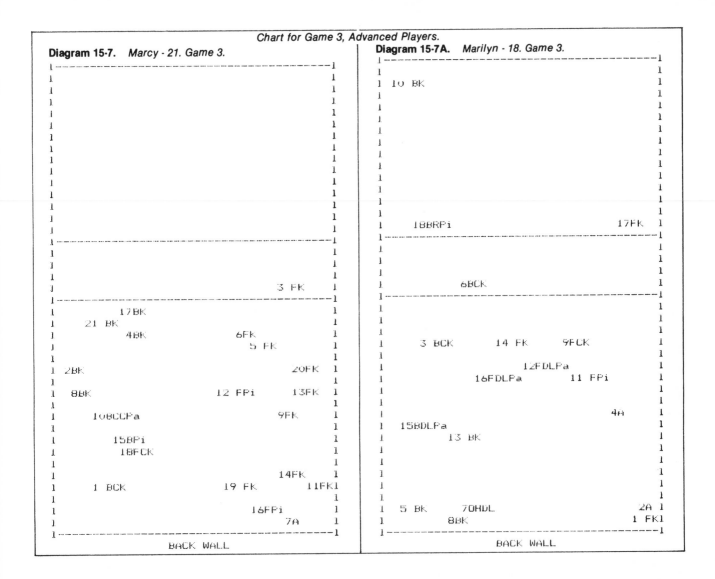

Diagram 15-7. *Marcy - 21. Game 3.*

Diagram 15-7A. *Marilyn - 18. Game 3.*

Learn a lesson from this match. Marcy's favorite game is to keep the opponent in the back court, by using crosscourt and down-the-line passes. When Marilyn neutralized the game, Marcy went to a weaker style of play and won.

Look closely at Marilyn's chart for game three. Marilyn passed Marcy four times while moving into front court (points 7, 12, 15, 16). Marcy lost three points because Marilyn moved well from back court to the front court to kill the ball (6, 17, 18).

Marcy had seven skips due to her high risk-style of play. Yet Marcy still won. Why? Because she is not a one-style player. She has a complete arsenal of shots, knows when to use them, and has the confidence to execute them. As you can see, adjustment in shot selection and strategy can win the match.

If you want to better your game and win more matches, charting will help channel your energies in a constructive direction. There is no easy road to victory.

Opponent's Strengths and Weaknesses				
Your Opponent's Weaknesses	Strategy Chart			
	Forehand Offensive	Backhand Defensive	Forehand Offensive	Backhand Defensive
Serve				
Return of Serve				
Rally				

Your Strengths and Weaknesses				
Your Repetoire of Shots	Strategy Chart			
	Forehand Offensive	Backhand Defensive	Forehand Offensive	Backhand Defensive
Serve	Z Jam Drive	Lob Overhead	Z Jam Drive	Lob Overhead
Return of Serve				
Rally				

CHAPTER 16

HOW TO WIN!

The game of racquetball is not hard to learn, but learning to win matches on a tournament level requires a commitment to self-improvement, and the ability to play a variety of styles. In short, you must learn what it takes to win by competing in both leagues and tournaments. The final result of these experiences will teach you the different strategies necessary to defeat various opponents.

Plan your strategy, but be able to strategically change your plan at will! Have you ever been in the lead 12 to 4 and lost 15 to 14? If so, you probably throught you had the game won and changed your strategy to a losing one. You should have a plan of attack for every style of racquetball, or, in other words, a strategy to defeat any type of opponent. Also, you must realize when your strategy is ineffective, and be able to effectively change your strategy at a moment's notice.

Your objective should be to form a game plan based on your opponent's strengths and weaknesses but within your limitations. The key idea is for you to **EXECUTE ACCURATELY!** If you know your opponent cannot cover a pinch shot, but you can't execute it effectively, don't attempt it.

KNOW WHAT YOU CAN DO

The first step is to list exactly what you can do within each phase of your game. **KNOW YOUR LIMITATIONS!** Be honest with yourself. Complete Tables 16-1 & 16-2. These tables should be used as a checklist for evaluating your racquetball skills. You should have reached 70 percent service accuracy before feeling that you have mastered a serve. This means 7 out of 10 Z-serves legally. The criteria for an effective service return is 70 percent. This means 7 out of 10 ceiling balls off of 10 drive serves. If you cannot kill 7 out of 10 returns of drive serves, do not list it as a return.

DISCOVER WHAT YOUR OPPONENT CAN DO

The next step is determining what your opponent's strengths and weaknesses are.

Table 16-1:	Checklist for Evaluating Racquetball Skills: Your Serve Capabilities	
Your Serve	Right Side of Court	Left Side of Court
Drive	no	yes
Z		
Lob		
Overhead		
Jam		

Table 16-2:	Checklist for Evaluating Racquetball Skills: Your Serve Return Capabilities	
Your Return of Serve	Right Side of Court	Left Side of Court
Drive	cb, pa	cb, ccpa
Z		
Lob		
Overhead		
Jam		

cb = ceiling ball, pa = pass, cc = cross court

Through charting, observation, or second-hand information, you can determine your opponent's weaknesses, then fill in the strategy on Tables 16-3 & 16-4 in order to formulate your game plan. Everyone will have strengths and weaknesses relative to his/her own game.

For example, you consistently win and score 15-10 against two different players. Your strength is to play the ball defensively, which keeps both players in back court and minimizes offensive opportunities. You also predict that the same two players would play each other evenly; however, player A usually dominates player B. The strength of player A is to cut the ball off and kill the ball towards the corners. The strength of player B is to pass down-the-lines. Player B's strength feeds player A's strength. The net result is more offensive opportunities for player A, which player B is too deep to cover. For player B to win, a change in playing strategy is necessary.

The preceding chapter offered a thorough explanation of charting. You can use these techniques to identify your and your opponent's strengths and weaknesses. Post this information into Table 16-3 and combine it with the information about yourself to formulate a strategy and game plan.

The following is an example of the kind of information that should be obtained from charting.

A. What serves does your opponent like to serve? Are they offensive or defensive, to the right or left side of the court?

B. What returns of serve will you use to counter the serves?

C. What returns of serve does your opponent favor (offensive or defensive)?

D. What serves will counter those favorite returns?

E. What pace does your opponent like in the rally (fast or slow)?

F. Does your opponent force the rally or wait for a good shot?

G. Where does your opponent like to position himself/herself during the rally?

H. What quadrant(s), areas off the court, during the rally are the opponent's weakest?

The following list is of common types of players and how to counter their strengths.

1. The one-arm bandit — usually a player who plays the entire court with the forehand. Play the backhand, occasionally hitting ceiling balls to the forehand corner and driving serves to both sides of the court.

2. The power player — use slow serves and hit ceiling balls, looking for unforced errors, and slowing the pace of the game.

3. The control player — hit drive serves and hit the ball as hard as possible, keeping the pace as fast as possible.

4. The out-of-shape player — give him/her a tour of the court. Move the poorly conditioned player from front to back and left to right, and when you sense that he/she is tired, bear down and keep the pressure on.

5. The psyche-out artist — ignore him/her completely.

6. Playing the pro — stay relaxed, be patient and hit your normal shots. A game is not time to be creative.

7. Playing the left-hander — play the backhand as much as possible, however, do not force

Table 16-3: *Opponent's Strengths and Weaknesses*

Your Opponent's Weaknesses	Strategy Chart			
	Forehand Offensive	Backhand Defensive	Forehand Offensive	Backhand Defensive
Serve				
Return of Serve				
Rally				

setups to the wrong side of the court. Take your normal shot and execute with confidence.

8. Playing the banger — a banger is a player who hits very hard but cannot kill the ball, be patient, do not force your shots, and sooner or later you will get the setup.

9. The aggressive player — likes to play close to the front wall looking for rekills; pass him/her silly.

PLAN A STRATEGY

Before selecting a strategy and the specific shots to implement that strategy, it is important to understand one basic concept: always deal from a position of strength. To understand this concept, four situations are discussed:

1. your strength vs. opponent's weakness
2. your strength vs. opponent's strength
3. your weakness vs. opponent's weakness
4. your weakness vs. opponent's strength

These situations have been arranged in preferential order. Situation 1 is the most desirable situation which can be applied to each aspect of the game, and should be heavily considered when you are formulating a strategy against every opponent. For example, (two right-handed players) player A's backhand is stronger than player B's backhand. Most of player A's forehand shots should go crosscourt to player B's backhand, and most of player A's backhand shots should be down-the-line to player B's backhand (situation 1). Should player A's shot travel crosscourt to player B's forehand, then situation 4 occurs.

SIMILAR SITUATIONS EXIST FOR THE SERVE, RETURN OF SERVE, AND RALLY. YOUR TASK IS TO IDENTIFY THIS STRENGTH VS. WEAKNESS CONCEPT IN EACH AREA OF BOTH OF YOUR GAMES. Translate this information into a workable strategy. Convert this strategy into a series of specific shots. You should then mentally prepare yourself prior to the match so that you can to implement this strategy and execute the shots accurately during the match.

STRATEGICALLY CHANGE YOUR PLAN

Never change a successful strategy, but always change a losing strategy. There is an old saying — "don't fix it if it ain't broke." This is the key premise for victory. However, many games are lost because what was successful at the beginning of a game didn't work throughout the entire game. A change in strategy is a good idea anytime your present plan becomes neutralized or ineffective. By neutralized. I mean that the opponent has countered and adjusted to your strategy and rendered it harmless. Ineffective means that you have selected the wrong strategy. Remember, faulty execution on

Table 16-4: *Your Strengths and Weaknesses*				
Your Repetoire of Shots	Strategy Chart			
	Forehand Offensive	Backhand Defensive	Forehand Offensive	Backhand Defensive
Serve	Z Jam Drive	Lob Overhead	Z Jam Drive	Lob Overhead
Return of Serve				
Rally				

your part doesn't mean that you should change your strategy, it means that you should execute your strategy better! Learn to know the difference.

You or your coach should be aware of three areas at all times during a match. These include the tempo change (fast or slow), stroke effectiveness (forehand or backhand), and attack posture (offensive or defensive). All three are equally important for your victory.

The first key area is the pace of each player relative to one another. Are both players in the same tempo? Are they at different tempos? One strategy is to change tempos on your opponent whenever opponent matches your tempo. If you started out fast and hot as a pistol for seven or eight quick points, and your opponent seems to be adjusting, change to a slow tempo. When the opponent adjusts down to your new pace, pick up the speed to take the game. This fast-slow-fast combination is an easy strategy to master and you should look for opportunities to initiate the change. The opposite situation can also occur; when the opponent seems hyped and intense, use a slow-fast-slow strategy to keep the opponent off balance.

The second key area to look for is stroke effectiveness. Are you executing properly with your forehand and/or backhand? Which of your opponent's strokes is damaging you most? Test the waters on both sides to find the answer, especially if you have never played this opponent before. If you feel that your opponent's backhand is a weak stroke, yet he/she is scoring points and controlling the game, be smart enough to realize that your

backhand is not up to the task, shift to a forehand strategy. During warm-up, watch for your opponent's poorer stroke technique to make itself known. Chances are 9 out of 10 that you will find the weaker hand if you study hard enough. However, when you are hitting your best serves and the opponent is rolling them out, don't hesitate to switch your serve to the opposite side, even if you are playing to the so-called stronger stroke.

The third key area is your attack posture: offensive-aggressive or defensive-patience. Ask yourself if you are scoring with your attack posture. If the answer is yes, continue in the same vein. If poor execution on your part is giving your opponent scoring opportunities, work on improving your execution. If the opponent is rolling your best shots and your so-called strategy, do an about-face and weasel him out of the victory.

Not many players can readily adapt game strategy and shot selection at will. Several reasons contribute to this serious failing: lack of ability; stubbornness; lack of self-confidence; lack of gray matter; or ego involvement to the point of refusing to believe the opponent can hit good shots.

GAME STRATEGY

String together the three key areas to form yourself a complete game plan. To simplify this terminology for both left- and right-handed players, forehand and backhand have been changed to right and left sides of the court, respectively. Pinpoint the game plan which will work best for you. Translate the

Table 16-5:	*Serve Selection*		
	Offensive	**Defensive**	**Opponent's**
Fast Pace	Drive Z Jam	Overhead Jam	Forehand
	Drive Z Jam	Overhead Jam	Backhand
Slow Pace	Z-Lob Waist-High Lob Overhead Lob	High Lob Half Lob	Forehand
	Z-Lob Waist-High Lob Overhead Lob	High Lob Half Lob	Backhand

Table 16-6: *Return of Serve Selection*

	Offensive	Defensive	Opponent's
Fast Pace	CC Pass/Kill Pinch	CC Ceiling Ball	Forehand
	Short Hop Down-the-line Kill	AWB Ceiling Ball	Backhand
Slow Pace	CC Pass Overhead Drive	CC Ceiling Ball	Forehand
	Ceiling Ball Down-the-line Overhead Drive	AWB Ceiling Ball	Backhand

a. CC-Crosscourt
b. AWB-Around-the-Wall Ball

Table 16-7: *Rally Selection*

	Offensive	Defensive	Opponent's
Fast Pace	Kill, Pinch Corner Kill Crosscourt Kill	Down-the-line Z-ball	Forehand
	Kill, Pinch Splat Crosscourt Kill	Down-the-line Z-ball	Backhand
Slow Pace	Overhead	Ceiling Ball *AWB	Forehand
	Overhead	*AWB Ceiling Ball	Backhand

*Around-the-Wall Ball

game plan dictated by the key areas into an actual shot selection. Practice all eight of these combinations until you can call on them at any time.

There are eight game strategies which are summarized from the key areas. A lot of time should be spent practicing each game strategy under game conditions. Regardless of the strengths and weaknesses of your practice partner, practice each strategy for an entire game. Mentally select the shots for each strategy and execute them at the correct time. Use them and rank your ability from highest to lowest (1 to 8), then improve your weakest strategy. The following is a list of those strategies:

1. Fast-Offensive-Right
2. Fast-Defensive-Right
3. Fast-Offensive-Left
4. Fast-Defensive-Left
5. Slow-Offensive-Right
6. Slow-Defensive-Right
7. Slow-Offensive-Left
8. Slow-Defensive-Left

Tables 16-5 to 16-7 convert the game strategies into specific shots.

MENTAL IMAGERY

Approximately one hour before the match, sit in a quiet place and plan your strategy. Select a service strategy, a return of service strategy, and a rally strategy. Use mental imagery to positively reinforce your game plan and then actually play the match in your head. See yourself serving every ace, returning every serve perfectly, and winning every rally. During pre-match warm up, practice these shots and mentally review your strategy.

EXECUTE YOUR PLAN! Use the ten seconds alotted for a serve to see each serve crack out. See yourself setup after the serve in the proper position. Select your opponent's return and see yourself rekilling the return. For example, mentally serve a drive serve to the right, envision yourself setup 3 ft. past the short line on the right side; when the opponent hits a down-the-line pass, you splat the ball off the side wall for a point.

Use the ten seconds when receiving to guess the serve. Watch the serve coming to you, mentally selecting the return from your game plan. Watch yourself execute the perfect shot, and then move to a position which covers the opponent's rally tendencies. For example, if you expect a Z-serve to the backhand, observe yourself cutting the ball off and hit a crosscourt pass shot. Move to 27 ft. and cover the opposite side.

Mentally repeat the rally strategy when the opportunity presents itself by selecting the shot (down-the-line pass). Reinforce your plan (down-the-line pass). There will be times when your plan becomes ineffective (your opponent covers the shot). You must recognize this immediately and change your plan (pinch the ball). **TAKE A TIME OUT TO REVIEW AND PLAN A NEW STRATEGY.**

EXAMPLES

Given: You are right-handed. Your opponent is right-handed, likes to play a fast pace, and shoots the ball hard at every opportunity. You suspect a backhand weakness. Select strategy 7 (slow-offensive-left) or 8 (slow-defensive-left), the difference being determined by the effectiveness of the opponent. You serve, they shoot, and you rekill; or you serve, they hit defensive, and you shoot.

Strategy: Serve Plan — Z-lobs and change-up lobs to the left side of the court.

Take a deep drop, protect against the pass and monitor the receiver's effective returns. If they shoot effectively, anticipate, and cover the front wall for rekills.

Return Plan — Ceiling balls to both sides of the court. Look for an offensive third shot by the opponent, cover for the rekill and don't get passed.

Rally Plan — Keep the opponent deep with Z-balls and down-the-line passes. Force him/her to shoot from back court, and cover for the rekill.

Given: You are right-handed. Your opponent is left-handed, and likes a slow-pace game. The opponent waits for a setup to shoot and relies on your position and weak crosscourt execution of backhand to exploit for winners. Select strategy 1 (fast-offensive-right) and 3 (fast-offensive-left).

Serve drives, Z's, and jams to both sides of the court. Use an offensive return of serve; however, don't give away points with poor crosscourt or pinch shots. Shoot straight kill shots down-the-line to bring the left-hander over to the left side of the court and setup future crosscourt shots. Short-hop the opponent's lob serves, keep the pressure on and don't let him/her setup. During the rally hit kills and splats, concentrate on fast occuring shots.

THE BOTTOM LINE IS THAT YOU MUST BE COMFORTABLE WITH MANY DIFFERENT STYLES OF PLAY AND ALSO BE FLEXIBLE ENOUGH TO VARY YOUR ATTACK AT THE PROPER TIME. Some people would disagree with my variable attack approach to the game, but I stand by it. You can see by the above examples how certain styles can match up to guarantee a victory. You must be smart enough to recognize that your style is causing your defeat, and then be able to change it. You've heard players say that they've got an opponent's number and can never lose to that opponent. However, by being able to vary your game strategy, you'll never have to give out your **NUMBER.**

HAVING THREE-TO-FIVE POSITIONS FOR EACH SERVE, TWO-TO-THREE RETURNS FOR EACH SERVE, THE ABILITY TO CHANGE THE TEMPO, AND THE SKILL TO DIRECT YOUR SHOTS INTO ONE AREA OF THE COURT WILL MAKE YOU THE COMPLETE PLAYER. Remember, only select the strategies which you can execute well during a game. A tournament is no place for creative racquetball. **PLAN YOUR VICTORY!**

CHAPTER 17

DOUBLES — THE LEGACY OF CHAMPIONS!

Gene Grapes has teamed with Al Schattner or Sam Caiazza to win five national racquetball doubles titles. They have also shared seven regional and seven state doubles titles in the open, seniors, and masters divisions. This legacy — by no means just another Horatio Alger story — is the story of a championship technique that is unique in utilizing brain power over brawn, while giving up nothing of the game's inherent excitement and slam-bang fun.

Championship doubles requires teamwork between the two individuals. A player who wishes to play good fundamental doubles must be as interchangable as parts on a fine automobile. A meshing of individual skills between each partner is absolutely essential for any success at all. Among these skills are communication, position during the rally, the serve and serve return, using a well-thought-out strategy to defeat your opponents, and a strong will to win.

DOUBLES IS A TEAM GAME! Without the skills I have listed, you and your partner are headed for disaster. To develop these necessary skills, you must: (1) Develop an average singles game; (2) Play with one partner for a long period of time; (3) Utilize good doubles fundamentals. This chapter will provide you with an understanding of the techniques and knowledge that are necessary to improve your chances of winning a championship somewhere down the road.

COMMUNICATION

Communication is probably the most important quality necessary to a good doubles team. Ideally, you and your partner should communicate so well that you actually play as one solid unit. Four periods of communication are most critical: before the match, while you are actually playing, during times out, and after the match. Prior to the match, discuss your general coverage patterns, offensive tactics, and which serves that you think will be effective. Try to anticipate your opponents' moves and how to successfully counter them. During the game, verbal signals should be loud and clear. Leave no doubt as to what should be done (i.e., "Mine," "Yours," "Switch"). Use your time out for communication or to stop the opponents' momentum. Plan countermoves against unexpected maneuvers.

After each match, review your performance with your partner. This will help you remember which moves worked well and where improvement is necessary. Be positive, encourage your partner and don't get down on one another. Never criticize each other on the court or in front of others. If your partner is playing badly, offer corrections quietly and calmly during a time out. Keep any criticisms you have completely constructive. Remember the golden rule; treat others as you would want them to treat you.

DRILLS

Doubles is a game which, by nature, requires a lot of practice of special situations which occur frequently during matches. Your partnership should include the drills which follow as part of your normal warm-up routine before each match. These drills will help your shot execution, familiarity with the power involved in a game situation, and the many adjustments in court position that might crop up.

FRONT COURT RALLY

Beginning players should position themselves at least three feet behind the short line on their respective sides of the court facing the front wall. Hit the ball hard across to your partner and prepare for the return shot. Concentrate on keeping your returns low and trying to regain your position after every shot! Keep this drill going as long as possible; then move to the other side of the court.

Intermediate players should also perform this drill, emphasizing killing the ball at every opportunity. A variation of this drill is to kill the ball down-the-line, then crosscourt, while your partner kills your crosscourt shot down-the-line. Let him then kill the ball crosscourt back to you.

Advanced players can increase this drill's difficulty by pinching the ball back and forth to one another. Use the same variations I listed for intermediate players. Kill the ball straight, then pinch it to your partner. Your partner can then kill it straight, and then pinch it back to you. Another variation is to kill the ball cross corner, then pinch it to your partner. Needless to say, all of these drills must be practiced by both partners from both sides of the court. Concentrate on all-important footwork; it is crucial to the game.

POSITION DURING THE RALLY

The I formation is the offensive/defensive alignment that places one team member up front to handle all kill-shot retrievals and rekills while the other partner floats in the back court. The back court player's responsibility can be easily attacked by four methods:

1. Move the back court player until he is exhausted. This will take the edge off his defensive game. The front court opponent will become ice cold, while you and your partner remain warm as toast.
2. Serve to the front court opponent, shoot the first ball before he/she can rush into front court.
3. Keep the ball low with down-the-line, pass shots, and pinch shots. Leave no chance for your opponents to make an effective return.
4. Use ceiling balls to force the deep player into the backhand corner until he makes a weak return. Then shoot the ball to the uncovered corner.

In my opinion, the side-by-side formation is much better than the I formation. Side-by-side will give you excellent coverage of the front court with each partner covering his or her own side. Side-by-side requires two quick individuals who can use their forehands to keep power drives from getting past them. The left-side player is forced to use the backhand up close and can be pounded unmercifully by V passes.

The majority of doubles players are right-handed. When a right-hander has to react to a fast shot, the tendency is to go crosscourt. Most hard drives in doubles then will go to the left side (crosscourt for a right-hander); a left-hander will rarely play the right side, so there is always a forehand covering drives on that side.

The right side player is then free to play closer to the short line.

Diagram 17-1 shows standard court positions for two right-handed players during the rally. Move to these positions as soon as possible after a serve.

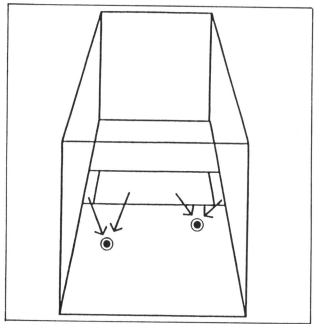

Diagram 17-1. *Court Position for Two Right-Handed Players.*

The rally position I have designed is to cover the pass shot and give you maximum court coverage. Each partner should move in unison as if tethered to the front wall through a pulley (Diagram 17-2). When one partner moves forward to play a shot, the other partner is drawn back in the opposite direction equi-

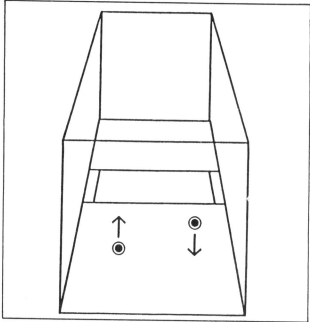

Diagram 17-2. *Partners Move in Unison as if They Were on a Tether.*

112

distantly to compensate. If your team acquires this ability, both of you will have an easier time of it. **RESTRAINT IS THE KEY!** Do not stab at a pass shot—let it go for your partner, who is covering you. **TRUST EACH OTHER.**

To win against opponents who play the correct position, hit around-the-world balls and Z-balls. Around-the-world balls and Z-balls should be hit softly and high so as not to come off the back wall. If you want to break your opponent's momentum, take a strategic time out.

Diagrams 17-3 & 17-4 show court coverage responsibility for two right-handed partners as the diagonal defense expands and contracts. The picture should resemble a modified L.

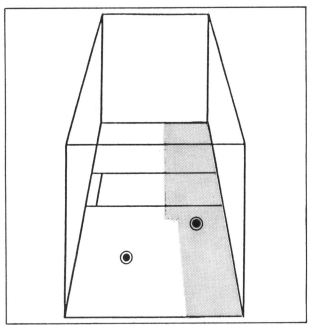

Diagram 17-3. *Court Cover Responsibility.*

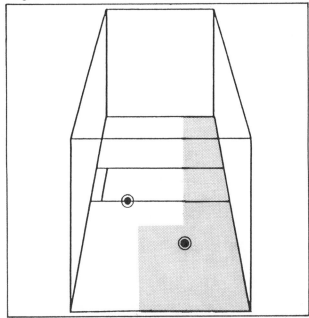

Diagram 17-4. *Court Coverage Responsibility.*

The lefty-righty formation shown in Diagrams 17-5 & 17-6 is designed to distribute an equal coverage area. The faster, stronger partner should be in the front position. You should move to the middle next to one another. Try to make it difficult for your opponents to exploit your backhand side. Look over your outside shoulder and be in the drop step position with your outside foot back. This will force your opponent to shoot to your forehand side. Avoid using your backhand, and you will deny center play to your opposition. I have used the modified L coverage pattern in this case.

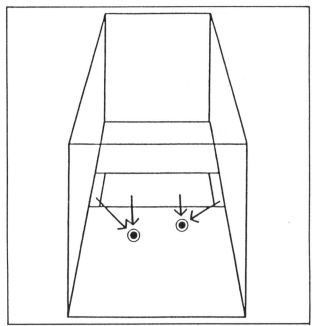

Diagrams 17-5,6. *Court Position for the Lefty-Righty Combination.*

The lefty-righty team has been proven to be the best combination for winning in doubles competition. Forehand shots can be hit down either side wall, and a good player can often run around a shot directed down the middle to pick up the forehand kill to the corner.

If the lefty-righty combination is the best, what can you do if you are not fortunate enough to find a southpaw partner, or if you and your partner are both lefties? Here are a few tactics which I use to defeat the lefty-righty team:

Try to create a situation where both members of the other team try for the same ball. Keep the ball low to their backhands, and use an angled shot if possible. Hit most of your serves to the middle. This will not only confuse the opposing team, but you may force them to use their backhands as well.

Here are some example situations:

1. Serve a low, hard drive up the middle. Be careful to keep this serve very low. Your

opponent will have time to adjust to a forehand if it comes off the back wall too forcefully.

2. Serve your medium speed Z-serve into the middle (7 and 8 feet up on the front wall). This will confuse your opponents and, since this is a slowly developing serve, keep the ball off the back wall.

3. The right side player should use pinch shots, crosscorner pinches, and low Z-shots into the left corner.

4. The left side partner should exploit the right side opponent and the middle of the court with angled shots (see Diagrams 17-17 & 17-18).

SERVING

In doubles competition, the movement of the offense and defense depends upon the path of the serve. Ideally, both teams should move to their respective formations as soon as possible after the serve. You should avoid serving from behind your back. Do not use your best serve all the time! Mix it up! Keep the opponents guessing! Imagine your serve perfectly hit, and practice the serve in your mind before execution. I have already explained how important the mental game is to winning in this game. Believe me, it's true!

Doubles serving is quite different from the serve in singles. Your serve should be higher and bring your opponents into a confused attempt to return the ball. You should attempt to serve mostly angular serves or serves which break into the middle (see Diagrams 17-7 to 17-14).

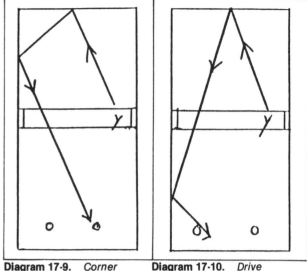

Diagram 17-9. *Corner Z-Serve.*

Diagram 17-10. *Drive Serve.*

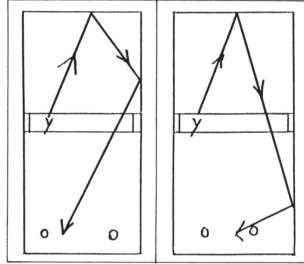

Diagram 17-11. *Overhead Z-Lob.*

Diagram 17-12. *Side-Arm Jam.*

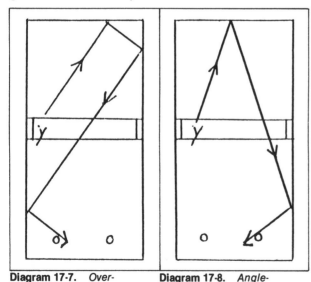

Diagram 17-7. *Overhead Z-Serve.*

Diagram 17-8. *Angle-Drive Serve.*

y = you, o = opponent, p = partner, • = ball

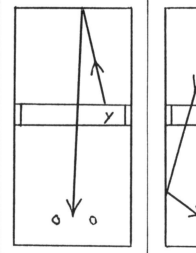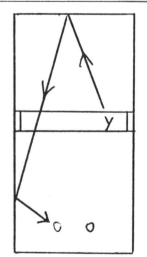

Diagram 17-13. *Middle Drive Serve.*

Diagram 17-14. *Overhead Angle Jam Serve That Breaks into Middle.*

RETURN OF SERVE

The serve in doubles will control the pace of the game. The serve also is often the deciding edge in winning the match. The return of serve then is the key factor to snatching victory from the jaws of defeat. Hit a safe return, a pass, or soft ceiling ball, then take front court position away from your opponents. Angle your returns, whenever you can. Your opponents will have an easier time covering your shots if you don't angle them.

Ceiling balls should be hit to the weakest point of the court, the left rear corner against two righties or middle of the court against a lefty-righty combination. Practice shooting ceiling balls which fall short or come off the back wall. Your opponents' rhythm can be broken, and the pace of the game will pick up if you force them to play the ball on the run.

The converse is also true. If your opponents gain control by using a fast pace, go to the ceiling and attempt to slow them down. The Z-lob served high and deep off the walls can also be used to slow their attack.

A good offensive strategy for the return of serve is for you to move up and cut the ball off on a fly. Your volley shot does not have to be a perfect pass or kill because your opponents will not have time to setup. **KEEP THEM ON THE RUN!** This is an especially good strategy during a rally when the opponents are positioned behind you.

Anticipate the return of serve by watching opponent's hitting motion and body movement. You should then form a mental image of where the serve will go and prepare for the volley return from midair. Against two righties use either the corner kill or the diamond pass shot. Against the righty/lefty combination, try to use the reverse pinch or low-Z shots up the middle.

The most common mistake many doubles players make is that they keep close to the walls after the serve. This will leave the middle wide open to be exploited by your opponent (see Diagram 17-15). Remember to coordinate your returns with your partner when he/she moves into the singles coverage position.

If the serve forces your partner deep, you should move temporarily into singles coverage, even if you are normally the deeper player. This will require you to play without the ball and stay in motion at all times (see Diagram 17-16).

RALLY

Gene Grapes believes that the key to winning every rally is your ability to determine

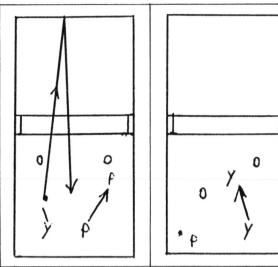

Diagram 17-15. *Return Down the Middle When Opponents Are Out of Position.*

Diagram 17-16. *Cover for Partner When He/She is Out of Position.*

your opponent's position, and your execution of specific shots to defeat this position (see Table 17-1). You can only consider yourself an advanced player if you have mastered every shot listed in this chapter and can use them at the proper time during a match. The beginning player should angle shots because the opponent will tend to cover straight shots more easily.

What should you do with the setup when you get it? The setup is defined as the shot which allows you the time necessary to position yourself to hit the best possible return with the highest probability of success. The fact is that both of your opponents must have a fair chance to get your shot. Your opponents can often claim unnecessary hinders simply because you did not hit your shot to the proper place. The following examples describe several common situations that happen all too often.

All four players are right-handed and a setup comes to your forehand in the middle of the court. What shot should you hit and where? The answer is to exploit your right side opponent's position. Why? Normally you cannot see the left side opponent. You can, however, see the right side opponent. Your partner should position himself/herself to determine the best return shot (Diagram 17-17).

If your opponent is in front of your partner, use a diamond pass shot to the right side or even better a reverse pinch shot into his/her backhand. When your partner is in front of the right side opponent, a straight kill or pinch will best exploit the right side opponent (see Diagram 17-18). The left side opponent must respect the power pass to the backhand even though the shot goes to the middle.

Table 17-1: *Your Opponent's Position*

		FRONT COURT	MIDDLE COURT	BACK COURT
YOUR POSITION ABOUT TO HIT THE BALL	FRONT COURT	Down-the-Line V Pass	Corner Kill Z-Ball Reverse Pinch	Pinch Shot Straight Kill Reverse Pinch Corner Kill
	MIDDLE COURT	V Pass Down-the-Line	V Pass Straight Kill Pinch Shot Reverse Pinch Corner Pinch	Straight Kill Pinch Shot Reverse Pinch Fly Kill Corner Kill
	BACK COURT	V Pass Down-the-Line Ceiling Ball Around-the-Wall Ball	V Pass Ceiling Ball Pinch Shot	Straight Kill Pinch Shot Reverse Pinch Overhead Drive

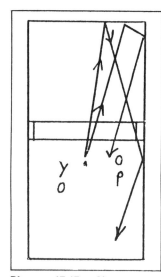
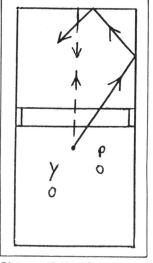

Diagram 17-17. *Shots to Exploit the Right Side Opponent.*

Diagram 17-18. *Shots to Exploit the Right Side Opponent.*

Do not confuse these situations with what some players use when a partner has a setup; they run in front of an opponent blocking their view, or inhibiting their movement to the ball. According to AARA rule 12 B, this is an avoidable hinder and you will lose your team a point or a serve if you violate it.

TIPS TO WIN THE RALLY

1. Develop a short, quick swing. Read chapter six.
2. Watch the ball until you have made contact. However, mentally form a line of direction in your mind, as to where you want the ball to go.
3. Let the ball drop for a kill shot. Your racquet frame may scrape the floor.
4. Move to a defensive position if your partner has a setup. This will allow you an excellent coverage position if the rally continues. If you get there first, your opponent will have to work harder for good court position.
5. Anytime you reach to the left for a backhand shot from the right side, your partner has more time to make a better shot with the forehand. In addition, the angle of the ball will usually give your partner an easier shot.
6. Watch your opponent on the opposite side. You have the responsibility to cover his/her shot.
7. Anticipate that every ball will come to you. Plan in your mind what shot and where you are going to shoot the ball.

8. If the ball comes directly at you in front court, you must make a quick decision on which way to move. Always move out of the way of the weaker shotmaker. This movement helps to take the stronger opponent away from the play.

9. Stay off the side walls during play. Control the middle.

10. Morale will improve if you protect your partner on the court. For example, if your partner is stranded in the front court, hit a ceiling ball to give him/her an opportunity to move back to safety. Help each other out!

11. Do not attempt soft shots.

12. Back off when you play a blaster (three feet).

13. Move up to your opponents when they have a setup. You want them to see you to increase the pressure. Do not, however, hit a defensive shot. You should then recover your normal position.

14. When you are alone in a front court rally against both your opponents, hit a defensive shot. Then recover your normal position as soon as possible.

15. Let shoulder-high balls go to the back wall. This will force your opponents to move out of the way. An easy setup will often result for you.

16. Cover your shot as well as your partner's shot. Follow your kill or pinch shot to the front wall.

STRATEGY TO DEFEAT THE OPPONENTS

The team that controls center court is the team that will win. When a team is caught in the back court, the front court team can easily cover kill shots. Most points in doubles competition are scored on kill shots because both players can easily cover their half of the court.

The front court team will always have the better visibility. Good vision is extremely important in doubles play because the game is so fast-moving. The team in the back court has got to pick out the ball through the four legs and four arms of their opponents in front court. This is not an easy task.

Playing the right side in a righty-righty combination will require a lot of patience from you. Your responsibility is to position yourself well, and to discourage shots into the right front corner. Try to force your opponent to play deep and over to the left side. Your partner will then have plenty of time to setup and work for a forehand offensive opportunity.

THE WORST THING YOU CAN DO WHEN PLAYING THE RIGHT SIDE IS TO STEAL YOUR PARTNER'S FOREHAND BY PLAYING A BACKHAND SHOT. Think offense! But — most of all — think! Don't beat yourself by playing too defensively, or mindlessly playing a ball your teammate would handle better.

For most experienced doubles teams, one partner will usually feel more comfortable and play better in the front court. You can usually attack this kind of team by serving to the front court opponent exclusively. If the front court opponent has to return your serve, then it will be much more difficult for the opponent to move into the front court. If your opponents use this tactic against **YOUR** team:

1. Hit a ceiling ball to give yourself time to move into the front court.

2. Take an aggressive service return position. Inch yourself up court and volley the return of serve past your opponent.

3. Alert your partner to take an extra step into center court to close up this zone. This will give you the protection to move forward later.

THE BEST TACTIC FOR DEFEATING THE CENTER-COURT STRATEGY AND WINNING THE MATCH IS THE ISOLATION THEORY! Top flight doubles, if played properly, is really two men against one.

You must decide where the point of attack is going to be before the match begins. Which of your opponents is the weaker player? What serves will you decide to use on them? Remember that both partners should serve to the weaker opponent, regardless of whether your best serve is to that side. How susceptible is your opponent to a little psychological stare? In some cases, the simple fact that an opponent knows he/she are being picked on can have an unraveling mental effect.

Avoid serving to the stronger partner at all times. The effect of this two on one strategy will be to deep-freeze the stronger opponent. The result will be two-on-one, and you will only need one-third of the court to win the game.

If you are unfamiliar with your opponents, assume that the weaker will always play the right side. This rule of thumb will also apply to two right-handers, and the lefty/righty combination. You must stay with your strategy throughout the entire first game. If you win, continue with that same strategy. If you lose the game, then reverse the point of attack and see if that works.

Remember that if your opponent is denied a shot for a long enough period of time, your opponent will be cold and your opponent's timing will not be as sharp when the ball does drift into their hitting zone. Eventually, the isolated player will become desperate to hit the ball. The player will then have a tendency to encroach on a partner's territory. A breakdown in teamwork will result, since neither opponent will know who is going to take what.

Morale will slump because the encroached-upon partner will begin to feel inadequate. The player who has been hitting all of the shots may start making overly aggressive shots and give you some easy points. The disenchanted teammate will then encroach even more to help out. This is the beginning of the end of that team!

The only effective defense against the isolation style of play is to hit the ball so that it becomes very difficult for your opponent to keep the ball in one particular area of the court. For example, use overhead drives, around-the-wall balls, and Z-balls, rather than sticking with the ceiling ball.

A ceiling ball rally is the easiest method of keeping the ball to the one isolated person. However, it will take tremendous poise and skill to take a well-hit overhead drive, around-the-wall ball, or Z-ball coming into your body and do anything more than just hit it.

As you plan your strategy, keep these things in mind: attack the backhand side, attack the weaker opponent, attack the defensive player, serve to the opponent who favors playing front court, and isolate the hot player.

THE WILL TO WIN

The will to win will require much more than simple drive and hustle from you. You must have poise, self-confidence, the ability to communicate, and the willingness to learn to play doubles correctly. When you have mastered all of these facets of the game, you will then be playing championship doubles.

Crossover Step.

BIBLIOGRAPHY

1. Auerbach, Marc and James L. Eager. PLAYING AND WINNING RACQUETBALL. Parker Publishing, West Nyack, N.Y., 1982, pp. 130-36.
2. Brumfield, Charles. "Inside the Master's Mind...The Serve Today: 25 Ways to Add Points to Your Score." NATIONAL RACQUETBALL, March, 1980, pp. 20-28.

    "Inside the Master's Mind," NATIONAL RACQUETBALL, August 1980, pp. 59-62.

    "Inside the Master's Mind," NATIONAL RACQUETBALL, November 1980, pp. 20-25.
3. Brumfield, Charles and Jeffrey Bairstow. ROLL-OUT RACQUETBALL. Dial Press: New York, 1982, pp. 70-71.
4. Csikszentmihalyi, Mihalv, BEYOND BOREDOM & ANXIETY, San Francisco, Ca.: Jossey-Bass, 1977.
5. Darden, Ellington, POWER RACQUETBALL, West Point, N.Y.: Leisure Press, 1981.
6. Fabian, Lou. "How To Make The Most Of Your Court Hour-Practice." NATIONAL RACQUETBALL, March 1982, pp. 24-30.

    "The Z-Serve." NATIONAL RACQUETBALL, June, 1982, pp. 26-30.

    "Anticipation — The Winning Edge," NATIONAL RACQUETBALL, December 1982, pp. 20-24.

    "Win More Through Charting!" NATIONAL RACQUETBALL, June, 1983, pp. 14-18.

    "Middle Court Play: Where The Game Was Won Or Lost (Part I)". NATIONAL RACQUETBALL, July 1983, pp. 22-24.

    "Middle Court Play: Where The Game Was Won Or Lost (Part II)." NATIONAL RACQUETBALL, September 1983, pp. 15-17.
7. Fabian, Lou and Molly O'Brian. "Training Aids For Racquetball - Part I." NATIONAL RACQUETBALL, October 1984, pp. 29-31.

    "Training Aids For Racquetball - Part 1." NATIONAL RACQUETBALL, November 1984, pp. 23-25.
8. Fabian, Lou and Gene Grapes. "Playing Doubles To Win! Part 1." NATIONAL RACQUETBALL, November, 1985, pp. 17-21.

    "Playing Doubles To Win! Part 2" NATIONAL RACQUETBALL, December, 1985, pp. 10-11.
9. Gallwey, Timothy W., THE INNER GAME OF TENNIS, New York: Random House, 1974, pp. 89-103.
10. Garfinkel, Charles. RACQUETBALL THE EASY WAY. Athenaeum/Smi, New York, 1979, pp. 67-71.

    RACQUETBALL FOR THE SERIOUS PLAYER, New York: Atheneum, 1982.
11. Jerome John, THE SWEET SPOT IN TIME, New York: Summit Books, 1980.
12. Keeley, Steve, THE COMPLETE BOOK OF RACQUETBALL, Chicago, Ill.: Follett Publishing, 1976.
13. Nideffer, Robert M., THE INNER ATHLETE, New York: Crowell Publishers, 1976.
14. Ornstein, Robert E., THE PSYCHOLOGY OF CONSCIOUSNESS, San Francisco, Ca.: W. H. Freeman Co., 1972.
15. Peck, Dave, "Using Your Eyes To Anticipate Your Opponent," TOTAL RACQUETBALL, San Diego, Ca.: EKTELON Inc., 1982, p. 61.
16. Stafford, Randy, RACQUETBALL: THE SPORT FOR EVERYONE, Memphis, Tenn., 1975.
17. Strandemo, Steve and Bill Bruns, THE RACQUETBALL BOOK, New York: Simon and Schuster, Inc., 1977.

    ADVANCED RACQUETBALL, New York: Simon and Schuster, Inc., 1982.
18. Williams, Kathy, SUCCESSFUL RACQUETBALL DRILLS, Denver, Co., 1983.